Mometrix
TEST PREPARATION

Regents

Success Strategies
Earth Science

I0880192

DEAR FUTURE EXAM SUCCESS STORY

First of all, **THANK YOU** for purchasing Mometrix study materials!

Second, congratulations! You are one of the few determined test-takers who are committed to doing whatever it takes to excel on your exam. **You have come to the right place.** We developed these study materials with one goal in mind: to deliver you the information you need in a format that's concise and easy to use.

In addition to optimizing your guide for the content of the test, we've outlined our recommended steps for breaking down the preparation process into small, attainable goals so you can make sure you stay on track.

We've also analyzed the entire test-taking process, identifying the most common pitfalls and showing how you can overcome them and be ready for any curveball the test throws you.

Standardized testing is one of the biggest obstacles on your road to success, which only increases the importance of doing well in the high-pressure, high-stakes environment of test day. Your results on this test could have a significant impact on your future, and this guide provides the information and practical advice to help you achieve your full potential on test day.

Your success is our success

We would love to hear from you! If you would like to share the story of your exam success or if you have any questions or comments in regard to our products, please contact us at **800-673-8175** or **support@mometrix.com**.

Thanks again for your business and we wish you continued success!

Sincerely,
The Mometrix Test Preparation Team

Printed in the United States of America

Table of Contents

Introduction

Thank you for purchasing this resource! You have made the choice to prepare yourself for a test that could have a huge impact on your future, and this guide is designed to help you be fully ready for test day. Obviously, it's important to have a solid understanding of the test material, but you also need to be prepared for the unique environment and stressors of the test, so that you can perform to the best of your abilities.

For this purpose, the first section that appears in this guide is the **Success Strategies**. We've devoted countless hours to meticulously researching what works and what doesn't, and we've boiled down our findings to the five most impactful steps you can take to improve your performance on the test. We start at the beginning with study planning and move through the preparation process, all the way to the testing strategies that will help you get the most out of what you know when you're finally sitting in front of the test.

We recommend that you start preparing for your test as far in advance as possible. However, if you've bought this guide as a last-minute study resource and only have a few days before your test, we recommend that you skip over the first two Success Strategies since they address a long-term study plan.

If you struggle with **test anxiety**, we strongly encourage you to check out our recommendations for how you can overcome it. Test anxiety is a formidable foe, but it can be beaten, and we want to make sure you have the tools you need to defeat it.

Strategy #1 – Plan Big, Study Small

There's a lot riding on your performance. If you want to ace this test, you're going to need to keep your skills sharp and the material fresh in your mind. You need a plan that lets you review everything you need to know while still fitting in your schedule. We'll break this strategy down into three categories.

Information Organization

Start with the information you already have: the official test outline. From this, you can make a complete list of all the concepts you need to cover before the test. Organize these concepts into groups that can be studied together, and create a list of any related vocabulary you need to learn so you can brush up on any difficult terms. You'll want to keep this vocabulary list handy once you actually start studying since you may need to add to it along the way.

Time Management

Once you have your set of study concepts, decide how to spread them out over the time you have left before the test. Break your study plan into small, clear goals so you have a manageable task for each day and know exactly what you're doing. Then just focus on one small step at a time. When you manage your time this way, you don't need to spend hours at a time studying. Studying a small block of content for a short period each day helps you retain information better and avoid stressing over how much you have left to do. You can relax knowing that you have a plan to cover everything in time. In order for this strategy to be effective though, you have to start studying early and stick to your schedule. Avoid the exhaustion and futility that comes from last-minute cramming!

Study Environment

The environment you study in has a big impact on your learning. Studying in a coffee shop, while probably more enjoyable, is not likely to be as fruitful as studying in a quiet room. It's important to keep distractions to a minimum. You're only planning to study for a short block of time, so make the most of it. Don't pause to check your phone or get up to find a snack. It's also important to **avoid multitasking**. Research has consistently shown that multitasking will make your studying dramatically less effective. Your study area should also be comfortable and well-lit so you don't have the distraction of straining your eyes or sitting on an uncomfortable chair.

The time of day you study is also important. You want to be rested and alert. Don't wait until just before bedtime. Study when you'll be most likely to comprehend and remember. Even better, if you know what time of day your test will be, set that time aside for study. That way your brain will be used to working on that subject at that specific time and you'll have a better chance of recalling information.

Finally, it can be helpful to team up with others who are studying for the same test. Your actual studying should be done in as isolated an environment as possible, but the work of organizing the information and setting up the study plan can be divided up. In between study sessions, you can discuss with your teammates the concepts that you're all studying and quiz each other on the details. Just be sure that your teammates are as serious about the test as you are. If you find that your study time is being replaced with social time, you might need to find a new team.

Strategy #2 – Make Your Studying Count

You're devoting a lot of time and effort to preparing for this test, so you want to be absolutely certain it will pay off. This means doing more than just reading the content and hoping you can remember it on test day. It's important to make every minute of study count. There are two main areas you can focus on to make your studying count.

Retention

It doesn't matter how much time you study if you can't remember the material. You need to make sure you are retaining the concepts. To check your retention of the information you're learning, try recalling it at later times with minimal prompting. Try carrying around flashcards and glance at one or two from time to time or ask a friend who's also studying for the test to quiz you.

To enhance your retention, look for ways to put the information into practice so that you can apply it rather than simply recalling it. If you're using the information in practical ways, it will be much easier to remember. Similarly, it helps to solidify a concept in your mind if you're not only reading it to yourself but also explaining it to someone else. Ask a friend to let you teach them about a concept you're a little shaky on (or speak aloud to an imaginary audience if necessary). As you try to summarize, define, give examples, and answer your friend's questions, you'll understand the concepts better and they will stay with you longer. Finally, step back for a big picture view and ask yourself how each piece of information fits with the whole subject. When you link the different concepts together and see them working together as a whole, it's easier to remember the individual components.

Finally, practice showing your work on any multi-step problems, even if you're just studying. Writing out each step you take to solve a problem will help solidify the process in your mind, and you'll be more likely to remember it during the test.

Modality

Modality simply refers to the means or method by which you study. Choosing a study modality that fits your own individual learning style is crucial. No two people learn best in exactly the same way, so it's important to know your strengths and use them to your advantage.

For example, if you learn best by visualization, focus on visualizing a concept in your mind and draw an image or a diagram. Try color-coding your notes, illustrating them, or creating symbols that will trigger your mind to recall a learned concept. If you learn best by hearing or discussing information, find a study partner who learns the same way or read aloud to yourself. Think about how to put the information in your own words. Imagine that you are giving a lecture on the topic and record yourself so you can listen to it later.

For any learning style, flashcards can be helpful. Organize the information so you can take advantage of spare moments to review. Underline key words or phrases. Use different colors for different categories. Mnemonic devices (such as creating a short list in which every item starts with the same letter) can also help with retention. Find what works best for you and use it to store the information in your mind most effectively and easily.

Strategy #3 – Practice the Right Way

Your success on test day depends not only on how many hours you put into preparing, but also on whether you prepared the right way. It's good to check along the way to see if your studying is paying off. One of the most effective ways to do this is by taking practice tests to evaluate your progress. Practice tests are useful because they show exactly where you need to improve. Every time you take a practice test, pay special attention to these three groups of questions:

- The questions you got wrong
- The questions you had to guess on, even if you guessed right
- The questions you found difficult or slow to work through

This will show you exactly what your weak areas are, and where you need to devote more study time. Ask yourself why each of these questions gave you trouble. Was it because you didn't understand the material? Was it because you didn't remember the vocabulary? Do you need more repetitions on this type of question to build speed and confidence? Dig into those questions and figure out how you can strengthen your weak areas as you go back to review the material.

Additionally, many practice tests have a section explaining the answer choices. It can be tempting to read the explanation and think that you now have a good understanding of the concept. However, an explanation likely only covers part of the question's broader context. Even if the explanation makes perfect sense, **go back and investigate** every concept related to the question until you're positive you have a thorough understanding.

As you go along, keep in mind that the practice test is just that: practice. Memorizing these questions and answers will not be very helpful on the actual test because it is unlikely to have any of the same exact questions. If you only know the right answers to the sample questions, you won't be prepared for the real thing. **Study the concepts** until you understand them fully, and then you'll be able to answer any question that shows up on the test.

It's important to wait on the practice tests until you're ready. If you take a test on your first day of study, you may be overwhelmed by the amount of material covered and how much you need to learn. Work up to it gradually.

On test day, you'll need to be prepared for answering questions, managing your time, and using the test-taking strategies you've learned. It's a lot to balance, like a mental marathon that will have a big impact on your future. Like training for a marathon, you'll need to start slowly and work your way up. When test day arrives, you'll be ready.

Start with the strategies you've read in the first two Success Strategies—plan your course and study in the way that works best for you. If you have time, consider using multiple study resources to get different approaches to the same concepts. It can be helpful to see difficult concepts from more than one angle. Then find a good source for practice tests. Many times, the test website will suggest potential study resources or provide sample tests.

Practice Test Strategy

If you're able to find at least three practice tests, we recommend this strategy:

Untimed and Open-Book Practice

Take the first test with no time constraints and with your notes and study guide handy. Take your time and focus on applying the strategies you've learned.

Timed and Open-Book Practice

Take the second practice test open-book as well, but set a timer and practice pacing yourself to finish in time.

Timed and Closed-Book Practice

Take any other practice tests as if it were test day. Set a timer and put away your study materials. Sit at a table or desk in a quiet room, imagine yourself at the testing center, and answer questions as quickly and accurately as possible.

Keep repeating timed and closed-book tests on a regular basis until you run out of practice tests or it's time for the actual test. Your mind will be ready for the schedule and stress of test day, and you'll be able to focus on recalling the material you've learned.

Strategy #4 – Pace Yourself

Once you're fully prepared for the material on the test, your biggest challenge on test day will be managing your time. Just knowing that the clock is ticking can make you panic even if you have plenty of time left. Work on pacing yourself so you can build confidence against the time constraints of the exam. Pacing is a difficult skill to master, especially in a high-pressure environment, so **practice is vital**.

Set time expectations for your pace based on how much time is available. For example, if a section has 60 questions and the time limit is 30 minutes, you know you have to average 30 seconds or less per question in order to answer them all. Although 30 seconds is the hard limit, set 25 seconds per question as your goal, so you reserve extra time to spend on harder questions. When you budget extra time for the harder questions, you no longer have any reason to stress when those questions take longer to answer.

Don't let this time expectation distract you from working through the test at a calm, steady pace, but keep it in mind so you don't spend too much time on any one question. Recognize that taking extra time on one question you don't understand may keep you from answering two that you do understand later in the test. If your time limit for a question is up and you're still not sure of the answer, mark it and move on, and come back to it later if the time and the test format allow. If the testing format doesn't allow you to return to earlier questions, just make an educated guess; then put it out of your mind and move on.

On the easier questions, be careful not to rush. It may seem wise to hurry through them so you have more time for the challenging ones, but it's not worth missing one if you know the concept and just didn't take the time to read the question fully. Work efficiently but make sure you understand the question and have looked at all of the answer choices, since more than one may seem right at first.

Even if you're paying attention to the time, you may find yourself a little behind at some point. You should speed up to get back on track, but do so wisely. Don't panic; just take a few seconds less on each question until you're caught up. Don't guess without thinking, but do look through the answer choices and eliminate any you know are wrong. If you can get down to two choices, it is often worthwhile to guess from those. Once you've chosen an answer, move on and don't dwell on any that you skipped or had to hurry through. If a question was taking too long, chances are it was one of the harder ones, so you weren't as likely to get it right anyway.

On the other hand, if you find yourself getting ahead of schedule, it may be beneficial to slow down a little. The more quickly you work, the more likely you are to make a careless mistake that will affect your score. You've budgeted time for each question, so don't be afraid to spend that time. Practice an efficient but careful pace to get the most out of the time you have.

Test-Taking Strategies

This section contains a list of test-taking strategies that you may find helpful as you work through the test. By taking what you know and applying logical thought, you can maximize your chances of answering any question correctly!

It is very important to realize that every question is different and every person is different: no single strategy will work on every question, and no single strategy will work for every person. That's why we've included all of them here, so you can try them out and determine which ones work best for different types of questions and which ones work best for you.

Question Strategies

☑ Read Carefully

Read the question and the answer choices carefully. Don't miss the question because you misread the terms. You have plenty of time to read each question thoroughly and make sure you understand what is being asked. Yet a happy medium must be attained, so don't waste too much time. You must read carefully and efficiently.

☑ Contextual Clues

Look for contextual clues. If the question includes a word you are not familiar with, look at the immediate context for some indication of what the word might mean. Contextual clues can often give you all the information you need to decipher the meaning of an unfamiliar word. Even if you can't determine the meaning, you may be able to narrow down the possibilities enough to make a solid guess at the answer to the question.

☑ Prefixes

If you're having trouble with a word in the question or answer choices, try dissecting it. Take advantage of every clue that the word might include. Prefixes can be a huge help. Usually, they allow you to determine a basic meaning. *Pre-* means before, *post-* means after, *pro-* is positive, *de-* is negative. From prefixes, you can get an idea of the general meaning of the word and try to put it into context.

☑ Hedge Words

Watch out for critical hedge words, such as *likely, may, can, often, almost, mostly, usually, generally, rarely*, and *sometimes*. Question writers insert these hedge phrases to cover every possibility. Often an answer choice will be wrong simply because it leaves no room for exception. Be on guard for answer choices that have definitive words such as *exactly* and *always*.

☑ Switchback Words

Stay alert for *switchbacks*. These are the words and phrases frequently used to alert you to shifts in thought. The most common switchback words are *but, although*, and *however*. Others include *nevertheless, on the other hand, even though, while, in spite of, despite*, and *regardless of*. Switchback words are important to catch because they can change the direction of the question or an answer choice.

⊘ Face Value

When in doubt, use common sense. Accept the situation in the problem at face value. Don't read too much into it. These problems will not require you to make wild assumptions. If you have to go beyond creativity and warp time or space in order to have an answer choice fit the question, then you should move on and consider the other answer choices. These are normal problems rooted in reality. The applicable relationship or explanation may not be readily apparent, but it is there for you to figure out. Use your common sense to interpret anything that isn't clear.

Answer Choice Strategies

⊘ Answer Selection

The most thorough way to pick an answer choice is to identify and eliminate wrong answers until only one is left, then confirm it is the correct answer. Sometimes an answer choice may immediately seem right, but be careful. The test writers will usually put more than one reasonable answer choice on each question, so take a second to read all of them and make sure that the other choices are not equally obvious. As long as you have time left, it is better to read every answer choice than to pick the first one that looks right without checking the others.

⊘ Answer Choice Families

An answer choice family consists of two (in rare cases, three) answer choices that are very similar in construction and cannot all be true at the same time. If you see two answer choices that are direct opposites or parallels, one of them is usually the correct answer. For instance, if one answer choice says that quantity *x* increases and another either says that quantity *x* decreases (opposite) or says that quantity *y* increases (parallel), then those answer choices would fall into the same family. An answer choice that doesn't match the construction of the answer choice family is more likely to be incorrect. Most questions will not have answer choice families, but when they do appear, you should be prepared to recognize them.

⊘ Eliminate Answers

Eliminate answer choices as soon as you realize they are wrong, but make sure you consider all possibilities. If you are eliminating answer choices and realize that the last one you are left with is also wrong, don't panic. Start over and consider each choice again. There may be something you missed the first time that you will realize on the second pass.

⊘ Avoid Fact Traps

Don't be distracted by an answer choice that is factually true but doesn't answer the question. You are looking for the choice that answers the question. Stay focused on what the question is asking for so you don't accidentally pick an answer that is true but incorrect. Always go back to the question and make sure the answer choice you've selected actually answers the question and is not merely a true statement.

⊘ Extreme Statements

In general, you should avoid answers that put forth extreme actions as standard practice or proclaim controversial ideas as established fact. An answer choice that states the "process should be used in certain situations, if…" is much more likely to be correct than one that states the "process should be discontinued completely." The first is a calm rational statement and doesn't even make a definitive, uncompromising stance, using a hedge word *if* to provide wiggle room, whereas the second choice is far more extreme.

⊘ Benchmark

As you read through the answer choices and you come across one that seems to answer the question well, mentally select that answer choice. This is not your final answer, but it's the one that will help you evaluate the other answer choices. The one that you selected is your benchmark or standard for judging each of the other answer choices. Every other answer choice must be compared to your benchmark. That choice is correct until proven otherwise by another answer choice beating it. If you find a better answer, then that one becomes your new benchmark. Once you've decided that no other choice answers the question as well as your benchmark, you have your final answer.

⊘ Predict the Answer

Before you even start looking at the answer choices, it is often best to try to predict the answer. When you come up with the answer on your own, it is easier to avoid distractions and traps because you will know exactly what to look for. The right answer choice is unlikely to be word-for-word what you came up with, but it should be a close match. Even if you are confident that you have the right answer, you should still take the time to read each option before moving on.

General Strategies

⊘ Tough Questions

If you are stumped on a problem or it appears too hard or too difficult, don't waste time. Move on! Remember though, if you can quickly check for obviously incorrect answer choices, your chances of guessing correctly are greatly improved. Before you completely give up, at least try to knock out a couple of possible answers. Eliminate what you can and then guess at the remaining answer choices before moving on.

⊘ Check Your Work

Since you will probably not know every term listed and the answer to every question, it is important that you get credit for the ones that you do know. Don't miss any questions through careless mistakes. If at all possible, try to take a second to look back over your answer selection and make sure you've selected the correct answer choice and haven't made a costly careless mistake (such as marking an answer choice that you didn't mean to mark). This quick double check should more than pay for itself in caught mistakes for the time it costs.

⊘ Pace Yourself

It's easy to be overwhelmed when you're looking at a page full of questions; your mind is confused and full of random thoughts, and the clock is ticking down faster than you would like. Calm down and maintain the pace that you have set for yourself. Especially as you get down to the last few minutes of the test, don't let the small numbers on the clock make you panic. As long as you are on track by monitoring your pace, you are guaranteed to have time for each question.

⊘ Don't Rush

It is very easy to make errors when you are in a hurry. Maintaining a fast pace in answering questions is pointless if it makes you miss questions that you would have gotten right otherwise. Test writers like to include distracting information and wrong answers that seem right. Taking a little extra time to avoid careless mistakes can make all the difference in your test score. Find a pace that allows you to be confident in the answers that you select.

⊘ Keep Moving

Panicking will not help you pass the test, so do your best to stay calm and keep moving. Taking deep breaths and going through the answer elimination steps you practiced can help to break through a stress barrier and keep your pace.

Final Notes

The combination of a solid foundation of content knowledge and the confidence that comes from practicing your plan for applying that knowledge is the key to maximizing your performance on test day. As your foundation of content knowledge is built up and strengthened, you'll find that the strategies included in this chapter become more and more effective in helping you quickly sift through the distractions and traps of the test to isolate the correct answer.

Now that you're preparing to move forward into the test content chapters of this book, be sure to keep your goal in mind. As you read, think about how you will be able to apply this information on the test. If you've already seen sample questions for the test and you have an idea of the question format and style, try to come up with questions of your own that you can answer based on what you're reading. This will give you valuable practice applying your knowledge in the same ways you can expect to on test day.

Good luck and good studying!

Earth Science

Theory of Plate Tectonics

PLATE TECTONICS

MAIN CONCEPTS

Plate tectonics is a geological theory that was developed to explain the process of continental drift. The theoretical separation of the Earth's lithosphere and asthenosphere is based upon the mechanical properties of the materials in the two respective layers and is distinct from the chemical separation of Earth's crust, mantle, and core. According to the theory of plate tectonics, the Earth's lithosphere is divided into **ten major plates**: African, Antarctic, Australian, Eurasian, North American, South American, Pacific, Cocos, Nazca, and Indian; it floats atop the asthenosphere. The plates of the lithosphere abut one another at plate boundaries (divergent, convergent, or transform fault), where the formation of topological features of Earth's surface begins.

THEORY

This theory of plate tectonics arose from the fusion of **continental drift** (first proposed in 1915 by Alfred Wegener) and **seafloor spreading** (first observed by Icelandic fishermen in the 1800s and later refined by Harry Hess and Robert Dietz in the early 1960s) in the late 1960s and early 1970s. Prior to this time, the generally accepted explanation for continental drift was that the continents were floating on the Earth's oceans. The discovery that mountains have "roots" (proved by George Airy in the early 1950s) did not categorically disprove the concept of floating continents; scientists were still uncertain as to where those mountainous roots were attached. It was not until the identification and study of the Mid-Atlantic Ridge and magnetic striping in the 1960s that plate tectonics became accepted as a scientific theory. Its conception was a landmark event in the field of Earth sciences—it provided an explanation for the empirical observations of continental drift and seafloor spreading.

TECTONIC PLATE MOTION

The two main sources of **tectonic plate motion** are **gravity** and **friction**. The energy driving tectonic plate motion comes from the dissipation of heat from the mantle in the relatively weak asthenosphere. This energy is converted into gravity or friction to incite the motion of plates. Gravity is subdivided by geologists into ridge-push and slab-pull. In the phenomenon of **ridge-push**, the motion of plates is instigated by the energy that causes low-density material from the mantle to rise at an oceanic ridge. This leads to the situation of certain plates at higher elevations; gravity causes material to slide downhill. In **slab-pull**, plate motion is thought to be caused by cold, heavy plates at oceanic trenches sinking back into the mantle, providing fuel for future convection. Friction is subdivided into mantle drag and trench suction. Mantle drag suggests that plates move due to the friction between the lithosphere and the asthenosphere. Trench suction involves a downward frictional pull on oceanic plates in subduction zones due to convection currents.

Review Video: Plate Tectonic Theory
Visit mometrix.com/academy and enter code: 535013

CONVERGENT PLATE BOUNDARIES

A **convergent** (destructive) **plate boundary** occurs when adjacent plats move toward one another. The Earth's diameter remains constant over time. Therefore, the formation of new plate material at diverging plate boundaries necessitates the destruction of plate material elsewhere. This process occurs at convergent (destructive) plate boundaries. One plate slips underneath the other at a subduction zone. The results of converging plates vary, depending on the nature of the lithosphere in said plates. When two oceanic plates converge, they form a deep underwater trench. If each of the converging plates at a destructive boundary carries a continent, the light materials of the continental lithosphere enables both plates to float above the subduction area. They crumple and compress, creating a mid-continent mountain range. When a continental plate converges with an oceanic plate, the denser oceanic lithosphere slides beneath the continental lithosphere. The result of such convergence is an oceanic trench on one side and a mountain range on the other.

Divergent Plate Boundary

A **divergent**, or constructive, **plate boundary** exists when two adjacent plates move away from one another. Observation of activity at diverging boundaries provided unquestionable proof of the seafloor-spreading hypothesis. At this type of plate boundary, kinetic energy generated by asthenospheric convection cells cracks the lithosphere and pushes molten magma through the space left by separating tectonic plates. This magma cools and hardens, creating a new piece of the Earth's crust. In the oceanic lithosphere, diverging plate boundaries form a series of rifts known as the oceanic ridge system. The Mid-Atlantic Ridge is a consequence of undersea diverging boundaries. At divergent boundaries on the continental lithosphere, plate movement results in rift valleys, typified by the East African Rift Valley.

Transform Plate Boundary

A **transform** (conservative) **plate boundary** exists when two tectonic plates slide past each other laterally and in opposite directions. Due to the rocky composition of lithospheric plates, this motion causes the plates to grind against each other. Friction causes stress to build when the plates stick; this potential energy is finally released when the built-up pressure exceeds the slipping point of the rocks on the two plates. This sudden release of energy causes earthquakes. This type of plate boundary is also referred to as a **strike-slip fault**. The San Andreas Fault in California is the most famous example of such a boundary.

Geologic Faults

A **geologic fault** is a fracture in the Earth's surface created by movement of the crust. The majority of faults are found along **tectonic plate boundaries**; however, smaller faults have been identified at locations far from these boundaries. There are three types of geologic faults, which are named for the original direction of movement along the active fault line. The landforms on either side of a fault are called the footwall and the hanging wall, respectively. In a **normal fault**, the hanging wall moves downward relative to the footwall. A **reverse fault** is the opposite of a normal fault: The hanging wall moves upward relative to the footwall. The dip of a reverse fault is usually quite steep; when the dip is less than 45 degrees, the fault is called a thrust fault. In the third type of geologic fault, the **strike-slip fault**, the dip is virtually nonexistent, and the footwall moves vertically left (sinistral) or right (dextral). A transform plate boundary is a specific instance of a strike-slip fault.

Features of the Earth's Crust

Geologic Folding

A **geologic fold** is a region of curved or deformed stratified rocks. Folding is one process by which Earth's crust is deformed. Rock strata are normally formed horizontally; however, geologists have identified areas where these strata arc upwards or downwards. **Anticlines** are upfolded areas of rock; downfolds are called synclines. In anticlines, the rocks are oldest along the axis (a horizontal line drawn through the point of the fold's maximum curvature), and in synclines, the youngest rocks are at the axis. **Monoclines**, or flextures, are rock structures that slope in one direction only, and often pass into geologic fault lines. The process of folding usually occurs underneath the Earth's surface, but surface erosion eventually exposes these formations. Folding is generally thought to be caused by the horizontal compression of the Earth's surface, which is related to the movement of tectonic plates and fault activity.

Orogenesis

Orogenesis refers to mountain-building processes, specifically as they relate to the movement of tectonic plates. An individual orogeny can take millions of years. Generally, mountains are created when compressional forces push surface rock upward, resulting in a landform that is higher than the land around it. There are four broad categories of mountains (which are not mutually exclusive); these categories are based on the mountain's formative origin. **Folded mountains**, formed from the long-term deformation and metamorphosis of sedimentary and igneous rocks, usually occur in chains. This type of mountain often forms at convergent plate boundaries. **Fault-block mountains** occur at normal or reverse faults with high dips. Portions of Earth's crust are vertically displaced along the faults. **Oceanic ridges** are formed at divergent boundaries beneath the ocean. When plates move apart, material from the mantle rises up and creates long mountain chains. **Volcanic mountains** form from the accumulation of products of volcanic eruptions, such as ash and lava. They often occur singularly, unlike other mountain types that usually exist in chains.

Continental Drift

Continental drift is a theory that explains the separation and movement of the continents based on shifts in a plastic layer of Earth's interior caused by the planet's rotation (seafloor spreading). Continental drift is part of the larger theory of plate tectonics. In the early twentieth century, many scientists and scholars noted that the edges of certain continents seemed to look like connecting pieces of a puzzle. Due to this observation, as well as the fact that similar geologic features, fossils, fauna, and flora existed on the Atlantic coasts of continents like South America and Africa, these observers theorized the previous existence of a supercontinent (referred to as Pangaea), in which all of the discrete continents identifiable today were joined together.

Continental Crust

The **continental crust** (sial) is 10–50 kilometers thick. It is more complex and locally variable than the oceanic crust. There is a correlation between the thickness of the sial and the age of the last orogenic (mountain-forming) event recorded at the surface: The thinnest crust occurs in areas of the oldest orogenic activity, and the thickest crust is located near present-day mountain chains. The continental crust consists of two layers separated by a seismic velocity discontinuity located 8–10 kilometers below the surface. The upper layer has an average density of 2,670 $\frac{\text{kg}}{\text{m}^3}$ and is composed mainly of granite. This layer exhibits thermal energy related to the activity of radioactive elements. The lower layer has gabbroic properties and an average density of 3,000 $\frac{\text{kg}}{\text{m}^3}$. The temperature of this layer is thought to be below the melting point of its component rocks and minerals and is extremely variable, depending on the presence of volatiles (elements such as water, carbon dioxide, and sulfur).

Oceanic Crust

The **oceanic crust** (sima) is 5–10 kilometers thick. It is remarkably uniform in composition and thickness and consists of a layer of sediments (fossils of marine life and continental debris) that overlies three distinct layers of igneous rock. The first of these is 1–2.5 kilometers thick and is made up of basaltic lavas. The second, main igneous layer is 5 kilometers thick and is of coarse-grained gabbroic composition. The third layer is very thin (less than half a kilometer thick) and possesses a density of 3,000 $\frac{\text{kg}}{\text{m}^3}$; this layer is made up of basalts. The temperature of the sima is very high along seismically active ridges and lower near oceanic basins. Based on dating of the fossils present in its sediments, scientists estimate that the oceanic crust is only 200 million years old (in comparison, the continental crust is estimated to be several billion years old). The relatively young age of the oceanic crust provides support for theories of the creative/destructive processes of seafloor spreading.

Magnetic Striping

Magnetic striping is a manifestation of the magnetic properties of the oceanic lithosphere. In general, the mineral composition of rocks has one of two magnetic orientations: normal polarity, which roughly corresponds with the polarity of the Earth's magnetic north, or reversed polarity, which is basically the opposite of the Earth's magnetic field. Cooled magma, which makes up the basalt of the ocean floor, aligns itself with Earth's current magnetic orientation during the cooling process. While the Earth's magnetic field normally shifts very slowly, it undergoes radical changes, called magnetic reversals, over long periods of time. Diverging plate boundaries on the ocean floor have been forming new crust material for tens of thousands of years, creating new midocean ridges throughout multiple reversals of Earth's magnetic field. Consequently, the ocean floor displays stripes of rocks with opposing polarities. The discovery of magnetic striping in the oceanic crust contributed to widespread acceptance of the seafloor-spreading hypothesis.

Seafloor Spreading

Seafloor spreading was originally put forth as an explanation for the existence of midocean ridges such as the Mid-Atlantic Ridge. These ridges were identified as features of a vast undersea mountain system that spans the globe. Seafloor spreading postulates that the ocean floor expands outward from these ridges. The process occurs when the upper mantle layer of the Earth (the asthenosphere), just beneath the planet's crust, is heated through convection. The heat causes the asthenosphere to become more elastic and less dense. This heated material causes the crust to bow outward and eventually separate. The lighter material then flows out through the resultant rift and hardens, forming new oceanic crust. If a rift opens completely into an ocean, the basin will be flooded with seawater and create a new sea. Often, the process results in failed rifts, rifts that stopped opening before complete separation is achieved.

Earth's Layers and Processes

Earth's Layers

Chemical Layers

The **crust** is the outermost layer of the Earth. It is located 0–35 kilometers below the surface. Earth's crust is composed mainly of basalt and granite. The crust is less dense, cooler, and more rigid than the planet's internal layers. This layer floats on top of the **mantle**. Located 35–2,890 kilometers below the Earth's surface, the mantle is separated from the crust by the **Mohorovicic discontinuity**, or Moho (which occurs at 30–70 kilometers below the continental crust and at 6–8 kilometers beneath the oceanic crust). The mantle is made up of rocks such as peridotite and eclogite; its temperature varies from 100 to 3,500 degrees Celsius. Material in the mantle cycles due to convection. The innermost layer of the Earth is the core, which consists of a liquid outer layer and a solid inner layer. It is located 2,890–6,378 kilometers below the surface. The core is thought to be composed of iron and nickel and is the densest layer of the Earth.

Sublayers

The **lithosphere** consists of the crust and the uppermost portion of the mantle of the Earth. It is located 0–60 kilometers below the surface. The lithosphere is the cooling layer of the planet's convection cycle and thickens over time. This solid shell is fragmented into pieces called tectonic plates. The oceanic lithosphere is made up of mafic basaltic rocks and is thinner and generally more dense than the continental lithosphere (composed of granite and sedimentary rock); the lithosphere floats atop Earth's mantle. The **asthenosphere** is the soft, topmost layer of the mantle. It is located 100–700 kilometers below the surface. A combination of heat and pressure keeps the asthenosphere's composite material plastic. The **mesosphere** is located 900–2,800 kilometers below the surface; it therefore spans from the lower part of the mantle to the mantle-core boundary. The liquid **outer core** exists at 2,890–5,100 kilometers below surface level, and the solid inner core exists at depths of 5,100–6,378 kilometers.

> **Review Video: Earth's Structure**
> Visit mometrix.com/academy and enter code: 713016

Cycling of Earth's Materials

Rock Cycle

The **rock cycle** is the process whereby the materials that make up the Earth transition through the three types of rock: igneous, sedimentary, and metamorphic. Rocks, like all matter, cannot be created or destroyed; rather, they undergo a series of changes and adopt different forms through the functions of the rock cycle. Plate tectonics and the water cycle are the driving forces behind the rock cycle; they force rocks and minerals out of equilibrium and force them to adjust to different external conditions. Viewed in a generalized, cyclical fashion, the rock cycle operates as follows: rocks beneath Earth's surface melt into magma. This **magma** either erupts through volcanoes or remains inside the Earth. Regardless, the magma cools, forming igneous rocks. On the surface, these rocks experience **weathering** and **erosion**, which break them down and distribute the fragments across the surface. These fragments form layers and eventually become **sedimentary rocks**. Sedimentary rocks are then either transformed to **metamorphic rocks** (which will become magma inside the Earth) or melted down into magma.

Rock Formation

Igneous Rocks: Igneous rocks can be formed from sedimentary rocks, metamorphic rocks, or other igneous rocks. Rocks that are pushed under the Earth's surface (usually due to plate subduction) are exposed to high mantle temperatures, which cause the rocks to melt into magma. The magma then rises to the surface through volcanic processes. The lower atmospheric temperature causes the magma to cool, forming grainy, extrusive igneous rocks. The creation of extrusive, or volcanic, rocks is quite rapid. The cooling process can occur so rapidly that crystals do not form; in this case, the result is a glass, such as obsidian. It is also possible for magma to cool down inside the Earth's interior; this type of igneous rock is called intrusive. Intrusive, or plutonic, rocks cool more slowly, resulting in a coarse-grained texture.

Sedimentary Rocks: Sedimentary rocks are formed when rocks at the Earth's surface experience weathering and erosion, which break them down and distribute the fragments across the surface. Fragmented material (small pieces of rock, organic debris, and the chemical products of mineral sublimation) is deposited and accumulates in layers, with top layers burying the materials beneath. The pressure exerted by the topmost layers causes the lower layers to compact, creating solid sedimentary rock in a process called lithification.

Metamorphic Rocks: Metamorphic rocks are igneous or sedimentary rocks that have "morphed" into another kind of rock. In metamorphism, high temperatures and levels of pressure change preexisting rocks physically and/or chemically, which produces different species of rocks. In the rock cycle, this process generally occurs in materials that have been thrust back into the Earth's mantle by plate subduction. Regional metamorphism refers to a large band of metamorphic activity; this often occurs near areas of high orogenic (mountain-building) activity. Contact metamorphism refers to metamorphism that occurs when "country rock" (that is, rock native to an area) comes into contact with high-heat igneous intrusions (magma).

Plate Tectonics Rock Cycle

The plate tectonics rock cycle expands the concept of the traditional rock cycle to include more specific information about the tectonic processes that propel the rock cycle, as well as an evolutionary component. Earth's materials do not cycle endlessly through the different rock forms; rather, these transitive processes cause, for example, increasing diversification of the rock types found in the crust. Also, the cycling of rock increases the masses of continents by increasing the volume of granite. Thus, the **tectonic rock cycle** is a model of an evolutionary rock cycle. In this model, new oceanic lithosphere is created at divergent plate boundaries. This new crust spreads outward until it reaches a **subduction zone**, where it is pushed back into the mantle, becomes magma, and is thrust out into the **atmosphere**. It experiences erosion and becomes **sedimentary rock**. At convergent continental plate boundaries, this crust is involved in mountain building and the associated metamorphic pressures. It is **eroded** again, and returns to the lithosphere.

Role of Water

Water plays an important role in the rock cycle through its roles in **erosion** and **weathering**: it wears down rocks; it contributes to the dissolution of rocks and minerals as acidic soil water; and it carries ions and rock fragments (sediments) to basins where they will be compressed into **sedimentary rock**. Water also plays a role in the **metamorphic processes** that occur underwater in newly-formed igneous rock at mid-ocean ridges. The presence of water (and other volatiles) is a vital component in the melting of rocky crust into magma above subduction zones.

METAMORPHISM

Metamorphism is the process whereby existing sedimentary, igneous, or metamorphic rocks (protoliths) are transformed due to a change in their original physiochemical environment, where they were mineralogically stable. This generally happens alongside sedimentation, orogenesis, or the movement of tectonic plates. Between the Earth's surface and a depth of 20 kilometers, there exists a wide range of temperatures, pressure levels, and chemical activity. Metamorphism is generally an **isochemical process**, which means that it does not alter the initial chemical composition of a rock. The changes a rock undergoes in metamorphism are usually physical. Neither a metamorphosing rock nor its component minerals are melted during this process—they remain almost exclusively in a solid state. Metamorphism, like the formation of plutonic rock bodies, can be studied only after metamorphic rocks have been exposed by weathering and erosion of the crustal rocks above.

FACTORS

Heat is a primary factor in metamorphism. When extreme heat is applied to existing rocks, their component minerals are able to recrystallize (which entails a reorganization of the grains or molecules of a mineral, resulting in increased density, as well as the possible expulsion of volatiles such as water and carbon dioxide). High levels of thermal energy may also cause rocks to contort and deform. **Pressure** is another factor affecting the metamorphism of rocks. Increased pressure can initiate recrystallization through compression. Pressure forces can also lead to spot-melting at individual grain boundaries. Lithostatic, or confining, pressure is created by the load of rocks above a metamorphosing rock. Pore-fluid pressure results from the release of volatiles due to thermal energy. Directed pressure is enforced in a certain direction due to orogenesis: This type of pressure is responsible for foliation, or layering, which entails parallel alignment of mineral particles in a rock, characteristic of metamorphism. **Chemical activity** affects metamorphism due to the presence of volatiles in pore fluids.

BIOGEOCHEMICAL CYCLE

The term biogeochemical cycle refers to one of several chemical processes in which chemical elements are (re)cycled among **biotic** (living) and **abiotic** (nonliving) constituents of an ecosystem. The theory of relativity necessitates the presence of such cycles in nature by virtue of its supposition that energy and matter are not created or destroyed in a closed system such as Earth's ecosystem. Generally, a **biogeochemical cycle** operates as follows: inorganic compounds, such as carbon, are converted from water, air, and soil to organic molecules by organisms called **autotrophs**. **Heterotrophs** (organisms that cannot independently produce their own food) consume the autotrophs; some of the newly formed organic molecules are transferred. Finally, the organic molecules are broken down and processed once again into inorganic compounds by secondary and tertiary consumers and replaced within water, air, and soil. Carbon, nitrogen, and phosphorus provide examples of nutrients that are recycled in the Earth's ecosystem.

Geologic Time and Earth's History

Uniformitarianism

Uniformitarianism is a basic tenet of the science disciplines. It states that the processes which made the world the way it is today are still in effect. This means that careful observation and analysis of the natural processes occurring right now can provide information about the processes which formed the world as it is now known. Simply put, it says that "the present is the key to the past."

An associated (but perhaps less generally accepted) idea is that of **gradualism**, which says that the processes which created the world as it is known operated at the same rate that they do now.

The doctrine of **uniformitarianism** is applicable in all scientific disciplines, from geology to the life sciences to astronomy to physics. In geology, uniformitarianism supplanted the theory of catastrophism, which suggested that earth was formed by isolated, catastrophic events, such as a worldwide flood.

Stratigraphic Correlation

The law of **superposition** states that in bodies of undisturbed sedimentary rocks, the strata at the bottom are older than the strata at the top. **Stratigraphic correlation** is a method used to determine the "correct" or natural stratigraphic position of rock beds which have been separated by disturbances such as metamorphic processes, orogenies, or plutonic formations. This is achieved through the identification of correspondence between two points in a characteristic such as fossil content, lithology (the physical characteristics of a rock), or geologic age. This practice of (theoretically) realigning beds which have been deformed is helpful in identification of the relative ages of rocks in a sedimentary rock sequence.

Important Terms

Geological stratum - a layer of rock which possesses certain attributes which distinguishes it from adjacent layers of rock. Such attributes include, but are not limited to, lithology, chemical composition, and mineralogy.

Stratigraphy - the study of the arrangement, form, distribution, composition, and succession of rock strata. Information gained from such study is then used to form hypotheses about the strata's origins, environments, relations to organic environments, relations to other geologic concepts, and ages.

Chronostratigraphy - an aspect of stratigraphy which focuses on the relative ages of geologic strata. Scientists examine the physical interrelations of strata, the relations of strata to the sequence of organic evolution, and radioactive ages of strata to determine their chronological sequence. When the relative ages of strata have been identified, scientists can examine the constituents and properties of those strata for clues about the sequence of events which made the world what it is today.

Record of the Earth's History

Rocks

One important way in which rocks provide a record of **earth's history** is through the study of **fossils**, which allows scientists to make inferences about the evolution of life on earth. However, the presentation of fossils is certainly not the only record of earth's history contained in rocks. For instance, the **chemical composition** of rock strata may give indications about the atmospheric and/or hydrospheric compositions at certain points in earth's history. Paleomagnetism constitutes another aspect of earth's historical record contained in rocks. Through the study of magnetic orientations of rocks formed at certain times in history, scientists learn more about the form and function of earth's magnetic field then and now.

Sediments

The study of the **sediments** which make up sedimentary rocks can reveal much about the environment in which they are formed. For example, a study of the **different types** of sediments in a bed, and the **ratios** in which they occur, can indicate the types of rocks exposed at the origination site and the relative abundances of each. Examination of the sorting of a sediment can reveal information about how far the particles traveled from their provenance, as well as the medium which carried the particles. For example, sediments transported by wind tend to be well-sorted, while water moves large particles which are often worn into spheres. The type of weathering experienced by particles in a sedimentary bed can reveal the climate from which they came—mechanical weathering tends to occur in cold and arid climates, while chemical weathering is more common in hot and humid climates. Interpreting the information supplied by sediment can, in turn, reveal information about past conditions on earth.

Soil

The study of **soil development** can give indications of the **age of certain sedimentary deposits**. For example, the study of soil led to the idea that multiple glaciations have occurred on the North American continent. Examination of the development level of certain areas of soil can also inform earth scientists about natural catastrophic events which have occurred in the past. Study of soil deposits also aided in the determination of how often "ice ages" can be expected to occur. Also, the presence of certain types of soil buried deep beneath the surface can provide indications of past climates.

Prehistoric Oceans

The elements present in the earliest oceans were quite different from those present in the Earth's hydrosphere today. This is largely due to the chemical composition of the atmosphere at that time. The oceans were formed when cooling caused atmospheric clouds to condense and produce rain. **Volcanic gasses** contributed elements such as sulfur and carbon dioxide to the air. Therefore, scientists suspect that the earliest oceans contained high levels of acids (for example, sulfuric acid, hydrochloric acid, and hydrofluoric acid), and low levels of the salts that inhabit the oceans today. The temperature in this early ocean was probably close to 100 degrees Celsius. As **carbon dioxide** began to dissolve in the water, it combined with carbonate ions to form limestone which was deposited on the ocean floor. Consequently, more carbon dioxide was trapped in these rocks. Eventually, **calcium carbonate** began to reduce the acidity of these early oceans. **Weathering** brought different minerals into the ocean, which began to increase its saltiness toward its current levels.

Radiometric Dating

Radiometric dating is one of the only methods currently available to determine the absolute age of an object such as a fossil or rock body. This process is possible when such an object contains isotopes, the products of radioactive decay. In radioactive decay, the atoms of certain unstable isotopes are transformed through the emissions of either electrons or alpha particles. This process occurs exponentially until it produces a stable final product. The rate of radioactive decay is measured in half-lives: after one half-life has passed, one-half of the atoms of the original element will have decayed. When scientists examine an object which contains isotopes with known half-life periods, they can determine the amount of the isotope that was present at the time of the object's origin. That figure can then be compared with the present level to determine the age of the object.

Gaia Hypothesis

Named for the Greek goddess who organized a living earth from chaos, the **Gaia hypothesis** states that the planet is a **living system**. While this idea is not scientific in the literal sense, it provides a metaphor which is useful in achieving an understanding of the interconnectedness of all of earth's systems. For example, increased levels of carbon dioxide in the atmosphere breed higher levels of plant growth, and these plants help to regulate the amount of carbon dioxide present in the atmosphere. Feedback mechanisms such as this were known before the formulation of the Gaia hypothesis. However, adherence to this idea requires one to study the planet as a whole, rather than focusing on only one of its many aspects in isolation. The fact that earth's atmosphere is quite different from those of the other planets led to the formulation of this idea.

Geologic Time

Geologic time may be measured absolutely using chronometric time, or relatively using chronostratic time. Measurements of chronometric time are achieved through **radiometric dating** and are expressed numerically in number of years. **Chronostratic time**, which places events in sequences, can be estimated through the study of rock bodies. According to the law of original horizontality, the original orientation of sedimentary beds is nearly always horizontal. Therefore, if one observes deformed or slanted strata, the event which disoriented the strata must have occurred after the strata were deposited. Also, a rock body that cuts across another must be newer than the rock body it intersects. Similarly, for a layer of rock to experience erosion and weathering, it must already exist on the surface. These destructive processes can lead to interruptions in the geologic record. Sometimes, sediments are deposited atop a weathered and eroded surface. Such an occurrence is called an unconformity. The most common method used to establish chronostratic time is through stratigraphy, as the name suggests.

Relative geologic time is divided into different units, including two recognized eons: the **Precambrian**, of which little is known due to limited fossil evidence that only reveals ultra-primitive life forms; and the **Phanerozoic**, for which fossil evidence is more abundant and reveals more evolved life forms. **Eons** are the largest units of geologic time.

Scientists also recognize three eras: the Paleozoic, the Mesozoic, and the Cenozoic. Eras contain periods, and periods contain epochs. These units are delineated largely by the conceptions used to divide historical time. They are arranged in a sequence through chronostratigraphy and classified largely on the basis of the fossils found in their associated strata.

Paleontology

Paleontology is the study of ancient plant and animal life. The bulk of information on this subject is provided by the fossil record, which consists of fossilized plants, animals, tracks, and chemical residues preserved in rock strata. There are three general subdivisions within the field of paleontology. The first, **paleozoology**, is the study of ancient animal life, including vertebrate and invertebrate specializations, as well as paleoanthropology, the study of fossil hominids. The second is **paleobotany**, the study of ancient plant life. The third, **micropaleontology**, is the study of microfossils. This field of scientific inquiry is useful in identifying the evolutionary processes that gave rise to present-day life forms. Paleontology also contributes to an understanding of the ways that environmental and geological factors affected evolution.

Evolution

Evolution is the process whereby organisms pass certain acquired traits to successive generations, affecting the attributes of later organisms and even leading to the creation of new species. Charles Darwin is the name often associated with the formulation of natural selection, a vital component of evolution as it is known today. **Natural selection** states that members of a species are not identical—due to their respective genetic make-ups, each individual will possess traits which make it stronger or weaker and more or less able to adapt. The other tenet of natural selection is that members of a species will always have to compete for scarce resources to survive. Therefore, organisms with traits which will help them survive are more likely to do so and produce offspring, passing along the "desirable" traits. Darwin suggested that this process, by creating groups of a species with increasingly different characteristics, would eventually lead to the formation of **a new species**.

Significant Events Leading to Evolution of Man

The **origination of life** is the most fundamental development in the history of life on Earth. Prokaryotic microfossils, the earliest fossils identified by paleontologists, are dated to near 3.5 billion years ago. However, the presence of large amounts of certain carbon and oxygen isotopes in sedimentary rocks dated at about 3.8 billion years ago may indicate the presence of organic material. The next significant event suggested by a drastic change in the fossil record is the huge diversification of species which occurred approximately 543 million years ago, near the end of the Precambrian eon and the beginning of the Phanerozoic. This theoretical evolutionary stage included higher-level tissue organization in multicellular organisms, the development of predator-prey relationships, and, most importantly, the development of skeletons. The final critical step toward the evolution of man is the emergence of life on land about 418 million years ago. This necessitated the evolution of structures which could breathe air, obtain and retain water on land, and support its own weight out of water.

Water Cycle and Energy Transfers Involved

Hydrologic Cycle

The **hydrologic (water) cycle** refers to the circulation of water in the Earth's hydrosphere (below the surface, on the surface, and above the surface of the Earth). This continuous process involves five physical actions. Evaporation entails the change of water molecules from a liquid to gaseous state. Liquid water on the Earth's surface (often contained in a large body of water) becomes water vapor and enters the atmosphere when its component molecules gain enough kinetic (heat) energy to escape the liquid form. As the vapor rises, it cools and therefore loses its ability to maintain the gaseous form. It begins to the process of condensation (the return to a liquid or solid state) and forms clouds. When the clouds become sufficiently dense, the water falls back to Earth as precipitation. Water is then either trapped in vegetation (interception) or absorbed into the surface (infiltration). Runoff, caused by gravity, physically moves water downward into oceans or other water bodies.

Evaporation

Evaporation is the change of state in a substance from a liquid to a gaseous form at a temperature below its boiling point (the temperature at which all of the molecules in a liquid are changed to gas through vaporization). Some of the molecules at the surface of a liquid always maintain enough heat energy to escape the cohesive forces exerted on them by neighboring molecules. At higher temperatures, the molecules in a substance move more rapidly, increasing their number with enough energy to break out of the liquid form. The rate of evaporation is higher when more of the surface area of a liquid is exposed (as in a large water body, such as an ocean). The amount of moisture already in the air also affects the rate of evaporation—if there is a significant amount of water vapor in the air around a liquid, some evaporated molecules will return to the liquid. The speed of the evaporation process is also decreased by increased atmospheric pressure.

Condensation

Condensation is the phase change in a substance from a gaseous to liquid form; it is the opposite of evaporation or vaporization. When temperatures decrease in a gas, such as water vapor, the material's component molecules move more slowly. The decreased motion of the molecules enables intermolecular cohesive forces to pull the molecules closer together and, in water, establish hydrogen bonds. Condensation can also be caused by an increase in the pressure exerted on a gas, which results in a decrease in the substance's volume (it reduces the distance between particles). In the hydrologic cycle, this process is initiated when warm air containing water vapor rises and then cools. This occurs due to convection in the air, meteorological fronts, or lifting over high land formations.

Precipitation

Precipitation is water that falls back to Earth's surface from the atmosphere. This water may be in the form of rain, which is water in the liquid form. Raindrops are formed in clouds due to the process of condensation. When the drops become too heavy to remain in the cloud (due to a decrease in their kinetic energy), gravity causes them to fall down toward Earth's surface. Extremely small raindrops are called drizzle. If the temperature of a layer of air through which rain passes on its way down is below the freezing point, the rain may take the form of sleet (partially frozen water). Precipitation may also fall in the form of snow, or water molecules sublimated into ice crystals. When clumps of snowflakes melt and refreeze, hail is formed. Hail may also be formed when liquid water accumulates on the surface of a snowflake and subsequently freezes.

Transportation of Water in the Water Cycle

In the **hydrologic cycle**, the principal movement of water in the atmosphere is its transport from the area above an ocean to an area over land. If this transport did not occur, the hydrologic cycle would be less a cycle than the vertical motion of water from the oceans to the atmosphere and back again. Some evaporated water is transported in the form of clouds consisting of condensed water droplets and small ice crystals. The clouds are moved by the jet stream (strong winds in the upper levels of the atmosphere that are related to surface temperatures) or by surface winds (land or sea breezes). Most of the water that moves through the atmosphere is water vapor (water in the gaseous form).

Review Video: Hydrologic Cycle
Visit mometrix.com/academy and enter code: 426578

Structure of the Atmosphere

Layers of the Atmosphere

The **atmosphere** consists of 78% nitrogen, 21% oxygen, and 1% argon. It also includes traces of water vapor, carbon dioxide and other gases, dust particles, and chemicals from Earth. The atmosphere becomes thinner the farther it is from the Earth's surface. It becomes difficult to breathe at about 3 km above sea level. The atmosphere gradually fades into space.

The main layers of the Earth's atmosphere (from lowest to highest) are:

- **Troposphere** (lowest layer): where life exists and most weather occurs; elevation 0–15 km
- **Stratosphere**: has the ozone layer, which absorbs UV radiation; elevation 15–50 km
- **Mesosphere**: coldest layer; where meteors will burn up; elevation 50–80 km
- **Thermosphere**: where the international space station and most satellites orbit; hottest layer; elevation 80–600 km
- **Exosphere** (outermost layer): consists mainly of hydrogen and helium; extends to ~10,000 km

Review Video: Earth's Atmosphere
Visit mometrix.com/academy and enter code: 417614

TROPOSPHERIC CIRCULATION

Most weather takes place in the **troposphere**. Air circulates in the atmosphere by convection and in various types of "cells." Air near the equator is warmed by the Sun and rises. Cool air rushes under it, and the higher, warmer air flows toward Earth's poles. At the poles, it cools and descends to the surface. It is now under the hot air, and flows back to the equator. Air currents coupled with ocean currents move heat around the planet, creating winds, weather, and climate. Winds can change direction with the seasons. For example, in Southeast Asia and India, summer monsoons are caused by air being heated by the Sun. This air rises, draws moisture from the ocean, and causes daily rains. In winter, the air cools, sinks, pushes the moist air away, and creates dry weather.

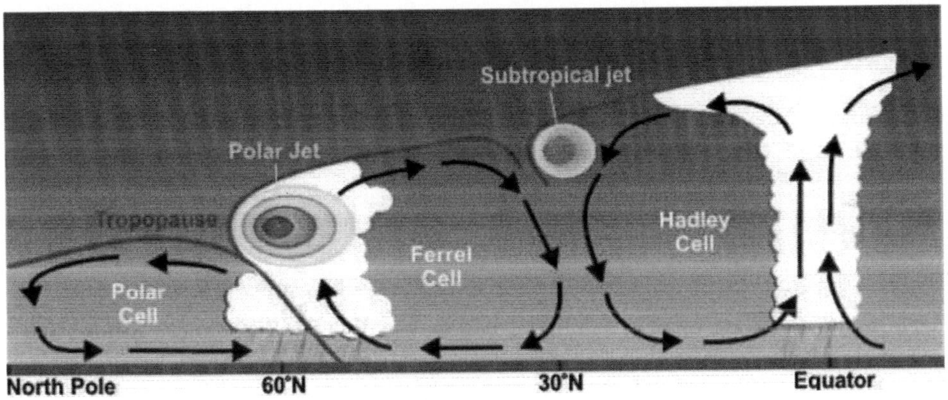

Weather Systems

WEATHER

Weather is the result of transfers of kinetic (heat) energy due to differences in temperature between objects as well as transfers of moisture in Earth's atmosphere. **Meteorology**, the study of weather, covers the same natural events as climatology, but observes them on a shorter time scale (usually no more than a few days). Rain, fog, snow, and wind are all examples of weather phenomena. The processes that occur at different stages in the hydrologic cycle form the basis of meteorological events. Most of the activity that produces the weather we experience on Earth takes place in the **troposphere**, the lowest level of the atmosphere. Atmospheric pressure, temperature, humidity, elevation, wind speed, and cloud cover are all factors in the study of weather.

Ozone Layer

The **Earth's ozone layer** is the region of the stratosphere with a high concentration of ozone (a form of oxygen) particles. These molecules are formed through the process of **photolysis**, which occurs when ultraviolet light from the sun collides with oxygen molecules (O_2) in the atmosphere. The ultraviolet radiation splits the oxygen atoms apart; when a free oxygen atom strikes an oxygen molecule, it combines with the molecule to create an **ozone particle** (O_3). Ozone molecules may be broken down by interaction with nitrogen-, chlorine-, and hydrogen-containing compounds, or by thermal energy from the sun. Under normal conditions, these creative and destructive processes balance the levels of ozone in the stratosphere. The concentration of ozone molecules in the atmosphere absorbs ultraviolet radiation, thus preventing this harmful energy from reaching the Earth's surface. Ozone particles form in the region of the atmosphere over the equator, which receives the most direct sunlight. Atmospheric winds then disperse the particles throughout the rest of the stratosphere.

Air Mass

An **air mass** is a body of air that exhibits consistent temperatures and levels of moisture throughout. These (usually large) pockets of air tend to come together under relatively still conditions, where air can remain in one place long enough to adopt the temperature and moisture characteristics of the land below it; this often occurs above wide areas of flat land. The region in which an air mass originates and the course of its motion are used to name it. For example, a maritime tropical air mass (denoted mT) is formed over the Gulf of Mexico (a tropical climate) and moves across the Atlantic Ocean (a maritime area). The conditions of an air mass will remain constant as long as the body is still, but when it moves across surfaces with different conditions, it may adopt those qualities. For example, polar air that moves over tropical land areas will be heated by the conditions below. Generally, maritime air masses contain high levels of moisture, and continental air masses are drier.

Meteorological Depression

A **meteorological depression** refers to a **low-pressure zone** (created by rising air) situated between 30- and 60-degrees latitude. These zones vary from approximately 321–3,218 kilometers in diameter. The rising air associated with a depression usually condenses at higher levels in the atmosphere and causes precipitation. Depressions are formed when warm air masses and cold air masses converge. At first, a single front (boundary between converging masses of air with different temperatures) separates the air masses.

A distortion similar to the crest of a water wave develops, creating a small center of low pressure. Then, differentiated warm and cold fronts develop from that center. A mass of warm air forms and rises over the body of cold air. The cold front and the cold air eventually catch up with the warm air, creating an occluded front and causing pressure to rise, effectually slowing the depression's movement. Depressions usually have life spans of four to seven days.

Prevailing Winds and Wind Belts

Wind (the horizontal movement of air with respect to Earth's surface) forms due to pressure gradients (differences) in the atmosphere. Air tends to move from areas of **high pressure** (such as the poles) to areas of **low pressure** (such as the tropics). Prevailing winds, or trade winds, are the winds (named in meteorology for the direction they come from) that blow most frequently in a particular region. For instance, the prevailing winds most common in the region from 90 to 60 degrees north latitude blow from the northeast, and are generally called the Polar Easterlies. Wind belts are created in areas where prevailing winds converge with other prevailing winds or air masses. The Inter-Tropical Convergence Zone (ITCZ), where air coming from tropical areas north and south of the equator come together, is an example of a wind belt.

Review Video: Source of Wind
Visit mometrix.com/academy and enter code: 451712

Coriolis Force

The **Coriolis force**, which gives rise to the **Coriolis effect**, is not really a force at all. Rather, it appears to be there to us because the Earth is a rotating frame of reference and we are inside it. In the atmosphere, air tends to move from areas of high pressure to areas of lower pressure. This air would move in a straight line but for the Coriolis force, which appears to deflect the air and cause it to **swirl**. Really, however, the Earth moves underneath the wind, which creates the impression of swirling air to someone standing on the Earth's surface. The Coriolis force causes winds to swing to the right as they approach the Northern Hemisphere and to the left as they approach the Southern Hemisphere.

Air Stability in the Atmosphere

Air stability is the tendency for air to rise or fall through the atmosphere under its own power. Heated air rises because it is less dense than the surrounding air. As a pocket of air rises, however, it will expand and become cooler with changes in atmospheric pressure. If the ambient air into which rising air ascends does not cool as quickly with altitude as the rising air does, that air will rapidly become cooler (and heavier) than the surrounding air and descend back to its original position. The air in this situation is said to be stable. However, if the air into which the warm pocket rises becomes colder with increased altitude, the warm air will continue its ascent. In this case, the air is unstable. Unstable air conditions (such as those that exist in depressions) lead to the formation of large clouds of precipitation.

Clouds

The four main **types of clouds** are cirrus, cumulous, nimbus, and stratus. A **cirrus** cloud forms high in a stable atmosphere, generally at altitudes of 6,000 meters or higher. Temperatures at these altitudes (in the troposphere) decrease with increased altitude; therefore, the precipitation in a cirrus cloud adopts the form of ice crystals. These usually thin traces of clouds may indicate an approaching weather depression. A cumulous cloud is a stereotypical white, fluffy ball. **Cumulous** clouds are indicators of a stable atmosphere, and also of the vertical extent of convection in the atmosphere—condensation and cloud formation begin at the flat base of a cumulous cloud. The more humid the air, the lower a cumulous cloud will form. A **nimbus** cloud is, generally speaking, a rain cloud. Nimbus clouds are usually low, dark, and formless, sometimes spanning the entire visible sky. A **stratus** cloud is basically a cloud of fog which forms at a distance above the Earth's surface. This type of cloud forms when weak convective currents bring moisture just high enough to initiate condensation (if the temperature is below the dew point).

The four cloud subtypes are cumulonimbus, cirrostratus, altocumulus, and stratocumulus. A **cumulonimbus** cloud is produced by rapid convection in unstable air. This type of cloud (which is often dark) is formed as a large, tall "tower." Collections of these towers (squall lines) often signal a coming cold front. Thunderstorms often involve cumulonimbus clouds. A **cirrostratus** cloud is an ultra-thin formation with a white tint and a transparent quality. An **altocumulus** cloud forms at an altitude from 1,980 to 6,100 meters. Clouds of this type, which appear to be flattened spheres, often form in clumps, waves, or lines. A **stratocumulus** cloud forms as a globular mass or flake. Stratocumulus clouds usually come together in layers or clumps.

Review Video: Types of Clouds
Visit mometrix.com/academy and enter code: 803166

Lightning

Lightning is a natural electrostatic discharge that produces light and releases electromagnetic radiation. It is believed that the separation of positive and negative charge carriers within a cloud is achieved by the polarization mechanism. The first step of this mechanism occurs when falling precipitation particles become **electrically polarized** after they move through the Earth's magnetic field. The second step of the polarization mechanism involves **electrostatic induction**, the process whereby electrically charged particles create charges in other particles without direct contact. Ice particles are charged though this method, and then energy-storing electric fields are formed between the charged particles. The positively-charged ice crystals tend to rise to the top of the cloud, effectively polarizing the cloud with positive charges on top and negative charges at the middle and bottom. When charged clouds conglomerate, an electric discharge (a lightning bolt) is produced, either between clouds or between a cloud and the Earth's surface.

Thunderstorms

A **thunderstorm** is a weather phenomenon that includes lightning, thunder, and usually large amounts of precipitation and strong winds. Thunder is the noise made by the rapid expansion and contraction of air due to the heat energy produced by lightning bolts. A thunderstorm develops when heating on the Earth's surface causes large amounts of air to rise into an unstable atmosphere. This results in large clouds of rain and ice crystals. The associated condensation releases high levels of heat, which in turn power the growth cycle of the cloud. The clouds created during thunderstorms are immense, sometimes reaching widths of several miles and extending to heights of 10,000 meters or more. The precipitation in such clouds eventually becomes heavy enough to fall against the updraft of unstable air; the consequent downpour is often short but intense. The differential speeds at which light and sound travel through the atmosphere enable one to estimate the distance between oneself and the storm by observing the interval between a lightning bolt and a thunderclap.

Hurricanes

Hurricanes form when several conditions are met: Oceanic water must be at least 26 degrees Celsius, the general circulation pattern of wind must be disrupted (this disruption usually takes the form of an atmospheric wave in the easterly trade winds), and the Coriolis force must be in effect. During hurricane season (June to November), easterly waves appear in the trade winds every few days. When such a wave occurs over a body of particularly warm, deep water, it is strengthened by the evaporation of warm air from below. Surrounding winds converge at the low-pressure zone created by the wave; air brought by these winds rises because it has nowhere else to go. The large body of warm, moist air rises high into the atmosphere and consequently condenses into huge clouds. As more and more humid air is drawn upward, this air begins to rotate around the area of low pressure. The storm continues to gain strength and may move toward land.

Tornado

A tornado is a violent rotating column of air that is in contact with both the ground and a cloud. The column is visible because the very low pressure causes water vapor to condense out as visible water droplets. Where the tornado touches the ground it usually stirs up a cloud of dirt and debris like the one in this photo. Tornadoes are the most violent storms on Earth, and the strongest spin at 300 miles per hour.

Review Video: Tornadoes
Visit mometrix.com/academy and enter code: 540439

El Nino

El Niño refers to the **unusual warming of surface waters** near the equatorial coast of South America. This phenomenon occurs during the winter approximately every two to seven years, lasting from a few weeks to a few months. El Nino can cause torrential rains, violent winds, drought, and dangerously high temperatures in surrounding areas. El Nino is caused by a reversal of the atmospheric pressures on the eastern and western sides of the Pacific (normally, pressure is high on the eastern side near South America and lower on the western side near the Indonesian coast). This reversal causes a wave of warm water to flow eastward and sea levels to fall on the western side. The changes in air pressure and ocean temperature cause moisture levels in the western Pacific to rise drastically while the region east of the Pacific experiences drought. The air pressure changes also weaken the region's trade winds, which normally serve to distribute heat and moisture.

Monsoons and Savannahs

The term **monsoon** refers to a unique pattern of moving air and currents that occurs when winds reverse direction with a change in season. India and Southeast Asia experience the most intense monsoons. This area lies between tropical and subtropical climate zones. During the winter season, northeasterly winds (which are generally dry) move from high-pressure subtropical areas to lower-pressure tropical areas. During the summer season, the continents of India and Asia heat up, creating a low-pressure zone. This causes winds to reverse and blow southwesterly across the Indian Ocean, accumulating high levels of moisture, thereby creating large amounts of precipitation during this season.

Savannahs also exist between wet equatorial and dry subtropical climate zones. These regions are characterized by vegetation consisting mainly of shrubs and grass. Savannahs experience dry weather throughout most of the year. A single, brief rainy season that occurs when the Sun is directly above the region interrupts prolonged dry spells.

Influence of Mountains on Climate

At the level of local climate, the presence of mountains forces air to rise to travel above them; this contributes to increased formation of clouds and consequently, increases in levels of precipitation. Mountain chains can affect regional and even global climates by deflecting airflow. The Coriolis force causes most of Earth's atmospheric airflow to move east and west. Therefore, the presence of north-south–oriented mountain chains can alter general circulation patterns. For example, the Rocky Mountains force air to move northward; the air cools near the North Pole before blowing back down. This causes winter temperatures in Canada and parts of the United States to be very cold.

Humidity and Cloud Cover

Humidity is a measure of the amount of water vapor in the air. **Specific humidity** is the expression of humidity as a ratio of aqueous vapor to dry air; it is expressed as a ratio of mass of water vapor per unit mass of natural (dry) air. **Absolute humidity** measures the mass of water vapor in a given volume of moist air or gas; it is expressed in grams per cubic foot or per cubic meter. The equilibrium (or saturated) vapor pressure of a gas is the vapor pressure (created by the movement of molecules) of water vapor when air is saturated with water vapor. **Relative humidity**, usually expressed as a percentage, is the ratio of the vapor pressure of water in air (or another gas) to the equilibrium vapor pressure. In other words, it is a ratio of the mass of water per volume of gas and the mass per volume of a saturated gas. Cloud cover refers to the amount of sky blocked by clouds at a given location.

Measuring Weather

Weather can be measured by a variety of methods. The simplest include measurement of rainfall, sunshine, pressure, humidity, temperature, and cloudiness with basic instruments such as thermometers, barometers, and rain gauges. However, the use of radar (which involves analysis of microwaves reflecting off of raindrops) and satellite imagery grants meteorologists a look at the big picture of weather across, for example, an entire continent. This helps them understand and make predictions about current and developing weather systems. Infrared (heat-sensing) imaging allows meteorologists to measure the temperature of clouds above ground. Using weather reports gathered from different weather stations spread over an area, meteorologists create synoptic charts. The locations and weather reports of several stations are plotted on a chart; analysis of the pressures reported from each location, as well as rainfall, cloud cover, and so on, can reveal basic weather patterns.

Global Warming

The **natural greenhouse effect** of the atmosphere is beneficial to life on Earth; it keeps temperatures on the planet 33 degrees higher than they would be without this phenomenon. Originally, this helped sustain life. However, it has been discovered in the last 20 years that this effect is being intensified by the actions of humans. In the twentieth century, certain activities of mankind, including the burning of fossils fuels like coal and oil, have resulted in an **increase in the levels of greenhouse gases** (such as methane and carbon dioxide) being released into the atmosphere. Also, increasing deforestation has affected the number of photosynthesis-practicing plants. The combined effect of these trends is a higher-than-normal concentration of greenhouse gases in the atmosphere. This, in turn, produces the effect of global warming. The average temperature at the Earth's surface has gone up 0.6 degrees Celsius in the last 100 years. Continuation of this trend is likely to have a detrimental effect on many of the planet's ecosystems, including that of human beings.

Earth-Moon-Sun System

Earth's Rotation

The **Earth rotates** west to east about its axis, an imaginary straight line that runs nearly vertically through the center of the planet. This rotation (which takes 23 hours, 56 minutes, and 5 seconds) places each section of the Earth's surface in a position facing the Sun for a period of time, thus creating the alternating periods of light and darkness we experience as **day and night**. This rotation constitutes a sidereal day; it is measured as the amount of time required for a reference star to cross the meridian (an imaginary north-south line above an observer). Each star crosses the meridian once every (sidereal) day. Since the speed at which Earth rotates is not exactly constant, we use the mean solar day (a 24-hour period) in timekeeping rather than the slightly variable sidereal day.

Sun

The **Sun** is the vital force of life on Earth; it is also the central component of our solar system. It is basically a sphere of extremely hot gases (close to 15 million degrees at the core) held together by gravity. Some of these gaseous molecules are ionized due to the high temperatures. The balance between its gravitational force and the pressure produced by the hot gases is called **hydrostatic equilibrium**. The source of the solar energy that keeps the Sun alive and plays a key role in the perpetuation of life on Earth is located in the Sun's core, where nucleosynthesis produces heat energy and photons. The Sun's atmosphere consists of the photosphere, the surface visible from Earth, the chromosphere, a layer outside of and hotter than the photosphere, the transition zone (the region where temperatures rise between the chromosphere and the corona), and the corona, which is best viewed at x-ray wavelengths. A solar flare is an explosive emission of ionized particles from the Sun's surface.

Review Video: The Sun
Visit mometrix.com/academy and enter code: 699233

Earth's Revolution Around the Sun

Like all celestial objects in our solar system, planet Earth revolves around the Sun. This process takes approximately 365 1/4 days, the period of time that constitutes a calendar year. The path of the orbit of Earth around the Sun is not circular but **elliptical**. Therefore, the distances between the Earth and the Sun at points on either extreme of this counterclockwise orbit are not equal. In other words, the distance between the two objects varies over the course of a year. At **perihelion**, the minimum heliocentric distance, Earth is 147 million kilometers from the Sun. At **aphelion**, the maximum heliocentric distance, Earth is 152 million kilometers from the Sun. This movement of the Earth is responsible for the apparent annual motions of the Sun (in a path referred to as the ecliptic) and other celestial objects visible from Earth's surface.

Review Video: Astronomy
Visit mometrix.com/academy and enter code: 640556

Review Video: The Solar System
Visit mometrix.com/academy and enter code: 273231

Seasons

The combined effects of Earth's revolution around the Sun and the tilt of the planet's rotational axis create the **seasons**. Earth's axis is not perfectly perpendicular to its orbital plane; rather, it is **tilted** about 23.5 degrees. Thus, at different times of the year, certain areas of the surface receive different amounts of sunlight. For example, during the period of time in Earth's orbit when the Northern Hemisphere is tipped toward the Sun, it is exposed to higher amounts of nearly direct sunlight than at any other time of year (days are longer, and the direction of Sun's rays striking the surface is nearly perpendicular). This period of time is summer in the Northern Hemisphere and winter in the Southern Hemisphere; on the opposite side of the orbit, the seasons are reversed in each hemisphere.

Review Video: Earth's Tilt and Seasons
Visit mometrix.com/academy and enter code: 602892

Summer and Winter Solstices

The **summer solstice** occurs when Earth's orbital position and axial tilt point the North Pole most directly toward the Sun. This happens on or near June 21 each year. On this day in the Northern Hemisphere, the Sun appears to be directly overhead (at its zenith) at 12:00 noon. The entire Arctic Circle (the north polar region above approximately 66.5 degrees north latitude) is bathed in sunlight for a complete solar day. The North Pole itself experiences constant daylight for six full months. Conversely, the **winter solstice** occurs when the South Pole is oriented most directly toward the Sun. This phenomenon, which falls on or near December 22 each year, orients the Sun as viewed from the Northern Hemisphere at its lowest point above the horizon.

Equinoxes

The **ecliptic** (the Sun's apparent path through the sky) crosses Earth's equatorial plane twice during the year; these intersections occur when the North Pole is at a right angle from the line connecting the Earth and the Sun. At these times, the two hemispheres experience equal periods of light and dark. These two points in time are respectively referred to as the vernal (spring) equinox (on or about March 21) and the autumnal (fall) equinox (on or about September 23). A calendar year is measured as the length of time between vernal equinoxes.

Moon

Earth's Moon is historically one of the most studied celestial bodies. Its mass is approximately 1.2% of the Earth's mass, and its radius is just over one-fourth of the size of the Earth's radius. Measurements of the Moon's density suggest that its characteristics are similar to those of the rocks that make up Earth's crust. The **landscape** of the Moon consists mostly of mountains and craters formed by collisions of this surface with meteors and other interplanetary materials. The Moon's crust (estimated to be 50 to 100 kilometers in thickness) is made up of a layer of regolith (lunar soil) supported by a layer of loose rocks and gravel. Beneath the crust is a mantle made up of a solid lithosphere and a semiliquid asthenosphere. The Moon's **core** (the innermost 500 kilometers of the body) is not as dense as that of the Earth. The Moon is made up mostly of refractory elements with high melting and boiling points with low levels of heavy elements such as iron.

Formation Theories

The **fission model** of Moon origin suggests that the Moon is actually a piece of the Earth that split off early during the planet's formation. In this model, a portion of the Earth's mantle fissioned off during a liquid stage in its formation, creating the Moon. According to the **capture model**, the Moon formed elsewhere in the solar system and was subsequently captured by the Earth's gravitational field. The **double-impact model** states that the Earth and the Moon formed during the same period of time from the same accretion material. Each of these theories has its strengths, but none of them can explain all of the properties of the Moon and its relationship to the Earth. Recently, a fourth (widely accepted) hypothesis has been suggested, which involves the **collision** between the Earth and a large asteroid. This hypothetical collision is said to have released a large amount of Earth's crustal material into its orbit; the Moon accreted from that material and the material displaced from the asteroid due to the collision.

EARTH-MOON SYSTEM

While the Moon is commonly referred to as a satellite of the Earth, this is not entirely accurate. The ratio of the masses of the two bodies is much larger than that of any other planet-satellite system. Also, the Moon does not truly **revolve** around the Earth. Rather, the two bodies revolve around a common center of mass beneath the surface of the Earth (approximately 4,800 kilometers from Earth's core). The **orbital planes** of the Moon and the Earth are nearly aligned; therefore, the Moon moves close to the ecliptic, as seen from Earth. Due to the Moon's synchronous rotation (its rotation period and orbital period are equal); the same side of the Moon is always facing Earth. This occurs because of the **mutual gravitational** pull between the two bodies.

PHASES

The **sidereal period** of the Moon (the time it takes the Moon to orbit the Earth with the fixed stars as reference points) is about 27 days. The **lunar month** (or synodic period) is the period of time required for the Moon to return to a given alignment as observed from the Earth with the Sun as a reference point; this takes 29 days, 12 hours, 44 minutes, and 28 seconds. A discrepancy exists between the two periods of time because the Earth and the Moon move at the same time. Sunlight reflected off of the Moon's surface at different times during the lunar month causes its apparent shape to change. The sequence of the Moon's shapes is referred to as the **phases of the Moon**. The full Moon can be viewed when the body is directly opposite from the Sun. The opposite end of the cycle, the new Moon, occurs when the Moon is not visible from Earth because it is situated between the Earth and the Sun.

CONFIGURATIONS

The **configurations of the Moon** describe its position with respect to the Earth and the Sun. We can thus observe a correlation between the phases of the Moon and its configuration. The Moon is at **conjunction** at the time of the new Moon—it is situated in the same direction as the Sun. **Quadrature** (which signals the first quarter phase) is the position of the Moon at a right angle between the Earth-Sun line; we see exactly half of the Moon's sunlit hemisphere. This is the **waxing crescent phase**, in which we see more of the Moon each night. Then comes opposition (which occurs when the Moon lies in the direction opposite the Sun)—we see the full Moon. After this point, the Moon enters its **waning gibbons phase** as it travels back toward quadrature. When it reaches that point again, it has entered the third-quarter phase. Finally, as the Moon circles back toward conjunction, it is in its waning crescent phase.

Review Video: Moon
Visit mometrix.com/academy and enter code: 880415

The Solar System

Terrestrial Planets

The term **terrestrial planets** refers to the four planets closest to the Sun (Mercury, Venus, Earth, and Mars). They are classified together because they share many similarities that distinguish them from the giant planets. The terrestrial planets have **high densities and atmospheres** that constitute a small percentage of their total masses. These atmospheres consist mostly of heavy elements, such as carbon dioxide, nitrogen, and water, and are maintained by the gravitational field of the planets (which could not prevent hydrogen from escaping). These planets exhibit magnetic fields of varying intensity. An important characteristic that distinguishes the terrestrial planets from the giant planets is the evidence of various levels of internally generated activity, which caused these planets to evolve from their original states. These processes are thought to have been caused by constant meteoritic impacts during the first few hundred million years of the planets' existence. Radioactive decay of certain isotopes increased the internal temperatures of these planets, leading to volcanic activity on all of the terrestrial planets except Venus.

Review Video: Terrestrial Planets
Visit mometrix.com/academy and enter code: 100346

Mercury

Mercury, the smallest interior planet, is the least well known of the four. This is due to its close proximity to the Sun and high temperatures. Mercury's atmosphere is not very dense; this means that the planet's surface experiences wide temperature differentials from day to night. Mercury's density is close to that of Earth. As the smallest planet known to have experienced planetary evolution, Mercury's internal activity ceased (it became extinct) thousands of millions of years ago. The size of the planet is relevant because less massive bodies cool more quickly than larger ones after cessation of radioactivity. Mercury's surface is characterized by craters produced by meteoritic impact.

Venus

Venus is comparable to Earth in both size and mass. Venus is the brightest planet in the sky, partially due to the fact that it is proximate to the Sun. This proximity to the Sun makes exploration of its surface difficult. This planet's atmosphere consists mainly of carbon dioxide, with trace amounts of water and carbon oxide molecules, as well as high levels of sulfuric, nitric, and hydrofluoric acids in the clouds that characterize this atmosphere. The concentration of clouds, coupled with the chemical makeup of Venus's atmosphere, result in a strong greenhouse effect at the planet's surface. This surface consists of large plains (thought to be created by either volcanic activity or by meteoritic impacts) and large impact craters. The materials that compose Venus's surface are highly radioactive. Some astronomers have suggested past single-plate tectonic activity; again, however, the planet's dense atmosphere makes valid surface observation quite difficult. Recent evidence points to the likelihood of current volcanic activity.

MARS

Mars and Earth exhibit many similarities. For example, Mars has an internal structure that includes a central metallic core, a mantle rich in olivine and iron oxide, and a crust of hydrated silicates. Martian soil consists largely of basalts and clay silicate, with elements of sulfur, silicon oxide, and iron oxide. The planet's surface belies high levels of past volcanic activity (though, due to its relatively small mass, it is probably extinct). In fact, Mars is home to the largest known volcano in the solar system. The Martian landscape also includes two major basins, ridges and plateaus, and, most notably, apparent evidence of fluvial (water-based) erosion landforms, such as canyons and canals. It is possible that the past pressures and temperatures on Mars allowed water to exist on the red planet. Some have gone so far as to suggest that this planet was a site of biochemical evolution. So far, however, no evidence of life has been found.

MARS'S SATELLITES

Two Martian satellites have been observed: **Phobos** and **Deimos**. Each of these bodies is ellipsoidal; the circular orbits of the two satellites lie in Mars's equatorial plane. The gravitational forces between this planet and Phobos and Deimos have caused both satellites to settle into synchronous rotation (the same parts of their surfaces are always facing Mars). This feature exerts a braking force on Phobos's orbit. In other words, its orbit is decreasing in size. The relationship between Deimos and Mars is similar to the Earth-Moon system, in which the radius of the satellite's orbit is gradually growing. The differential compositions and densities of Mars and its satellites indicate that Phobos and Deimos probably did not break off from Mars.

GIANT PLANETS

The **large diameters** of Jupiter, Saturn, Uranus, and Neptune gave rise to the name of the category into which they fall. The **hypothetical icy cores** of these planets cause them to exhibit primary atmospheres, because the large levels of mass they accreted prevented even the lightest elements from escaping their gravitational pulls. The atmospheres of the giant planets thus consist mostly of hydrogen and helium. The giant planets do not have solid surfaces like those of the terrestrial planets. Jupiter probably consists of a core (made of ice and rock) surrounded by a layer of metallic hydrogen, which is covered by a convective atmosphere of hydrogen and helium. Saturn is believed to have the same type of core and hydrogen mantle, enriched by the helium missing from the atmosphere, surrounded by a differentiation zone and a hydrogenic atmosphere. Uranus and Neptune probably have the same type of core, surrounded by ionic materials, bounded by methane-rich molecular envelopes. Uranus is the only giant planet that exhibits no evidence of internal activity.

Review Video: Giant Planets
Visit mometrix.com/academy and enter code: 563115

RINGS

Each of the four giant planets exhibits **rings**. These are flat disks of fragmented material that orbit just next to their respective planets. Many of the giant planets' smaller satellites are embedded in these rings. There are two main hypotheses regarding the formation of such rings. One theory suggests that the tidal force exerted on a satellite by its planet may surpass the **Roche limit** (the point at which particle cohesion is no longer possible) and break the satellite into fragments, which then collide and become smaller. This material then spreads out and forms a ring. An alternate theory of the formation of the rings of the giant planets suggests that there was unaccreted material left over after the formation of these planets. Below the Roche limit (within a certain vicinity to the planet), these particles could not join together to form satellites and would consequently settle into orbital rings.

SATELLITES

Each of the giant planets possesses a number of **satellites. Jupiter** has over 50 known satellites—they are grouped according to size. Each of the four largest satellites of Jupiter exhibits evidence of internal activity at some point in their evolutions. In fact, Io, the densest satellite and the one closest to Jupiter, is the only celestial body besides Earth known to be currently volcanically active. **Saturn** has 21 satellites. Titan, the second-largest known satellite, has its own atmosphere. The other six largest of Saturn's satellites all have icy surfaces; some of these show evidence of past internal activity. The smaller 14 are relatively unknown. **Uranus** has five satellites. Each of them displays evidence of geological activity, in the form of valleys, smoothed surfaces, cliffs, mountains, and depressions. **Neptune** has eight known satellites. The larger, Triton, is similar to Titan in that it has an atmosphere. The other seven satellites of Neptune are relatively unknown.

PLUTO AND CHARON

Though Charon was originally considered a satellite of Pluto, it now appears that the two are more accurately described as a double dwarf planet system (largely because of the similarity in the sizes of the two and the recurring debate over how Pluto should be classified). It is believed that these bodies formed from the solar nebula like most other objects in the solar system. Pluto has a highly irregular orbit, which places it closer to the Sun than Neptune for periods of time. In sharp contrast to its giant neighbors, this planet's density is higher than that of water ice. The surface of Pluto consists of high levels of methane absorbed into ice, with trace amounts of carbon oxide and nitrogen. Charon resembles the major Uranian satellites more so than it does Pluto. It consists of water ice with a siliceous or hydrocarbonate contaminant.

Review Video: Pluto and Charon
Visit mometrix.com/academy and enter code: 426296

KEPLER'S LAWS

Kepler's laws are a collection of observations about the motion of planets in the solar system. Formulated by Johannes Kepler in the 1600s, these laws are still vital to our understanding of the way the universe works. **Kepler's first law** states that each planet moves in its own elliptical path and that all of these orbits have the Sun as their singular focal point. Before Kepler's discovery, astronomers had assumed that planetary orbits were circular (because the heavens were assumed to be geometrically perfect). **Kepler's second law** says that a straight line between a planet and the Sun sweeps out equal areas in equal time. In other words, planets move quickest in the part of their orbit that is closest to the Sun, and vice versa. **Kepler's third law** states that the further a planet is from the Sun, the longer its orbital period will be. In mathematical terms, the square of a planet's period is directly proportional to the cube of the radius of its orbit.

Stars and Other Objects in Space

Stellar Observation

The observation of stars relates to one of three stellar properties: position, brightness, and spectra. **Positional stellar observation** is principally performed through study of the positions of stars on multiple photographic plates. Historically, this type of analysis was done through measurement of the angular positions of the stars in the sky. **Parallax** of a star is its apparent shift in position due to the revolution of the Earth about the Sun; this property can be used to establish the distance to a star. Observation of the **brightness** of a star involves the categorization of stars according to their magnitudes. There is a fixed intensity ratio between each of the six magnitudes. Since stars emit light over a range of wavelengths, viewing a star at different wavelengths can give an indication of its temperature. The analysis of stars' **spectra** provides information about the temperatures of stars—the higher a star's temperature, the more ionized the gas in its outer layer. A star's spectrum also relates to its chemical composition.

Binary Star

Binary star systems, of which about fifty percent of the stars in the sky are members, consist of two stars that orbit each other. The orbits of and distances between members of a binary system vary. A **visual binary** is a pair of stars that can be visually observed. Positional measurements of a visual binary reveal the orbital paths of the two stars. Astronomers can identify astrometric binaries through long-term observation of a visible star—if the star appears to wobble, it may be inferred that it is orbiting a companion star that is not visible. An **eclipsing binary** can be identified through observation of the brightness of a star. Variations in the visual brightness of a star can occur when one star in a binary system passes in front of the other. Sometimes, variations in the spectral lines of a star occur because it is in a binary system. This type of binary is a spectroscopic binary.

Review Video: Types of Stars
Visit mometrix.com/academy and enter code: 831934

Hertzsprung-Russell Diagram

The **Hertzsprung-Russell (H-R) diagram** was developed to explore the relationships between the luminosities and spectral qualities of stars. This diagram involves plotting these qualities on a graph, with absolute magnitude (luminosity) on the vertical and spectral class on the horizontal. Plotting a number of stars on the H-R diagram demonstrates that stars fall into narrowly defined regions, which correspond to stages in stellar evolution. Most stars are situated in a diagonal strip that runs from the top-left (high temperature, high luminosity) to the lower-right (low temperature, low luminosity). This diagonal line shows stars in the main sequence of evolution (often called dwarfs). Stars that fall above this line on the diagram (low temperature, high luminosity) are believed to be much larger than the stars on the main sequence (because their high luminosities are not due to higher temperatures than main sequence stars); they are termed giants and supergiants. Stars below the main sequence (high temperature, low luminosity) are called white dwarfs. The H-R diagram is useful in calculating distances to stars.

Stellar Evolution

The life cycle of a star is closely related to its **mass**—low-mass stars become white dwarfs, while high-mass stars become **supernovae**. A star is born when a **protostar** is formed from a **collapsing interstellar cloud**. The temperature at the center of the protostar rises, allowing nucleosynthesis to begin. **Nucleosynthesis**, or hydrogen-burning through fusion, entails a release of energy.

Eventually, the star runs out of fuel (hydrogen). If the star is relatively low mass, the disruption of hydrostatic equilibrium allows the star to contract due to gravity. This raises the temperature just outside the core to a point at which nucleosynthesis and a different kind of fusion (with helium as fuel) that produces a carbon nucleus can occur. The star swells with greater energy, becoming a red giant. Once this phase is over, gravity becomes active again, shrinking the star until the degeneracy pressure of electrons begins to operate, creating a white dwarf that will eventually burn out. If the star has a high mass, the depletion of hydrogen creates a supernova.

SUPERNOVA

When a star on the main sequence runs out of hydrogen fuel, it begins to burn helium (the by-product of nucleosynthesis). Once helium-burning is complete in a massive star, the mass causes the core temperature to rise, enabling the fusion of carbon, then silicon, and a succession of other atomic nuclei, each of which takes place in a new shell further out of the core. When the fusion cycle reaches iron (which cannot serve as fuel for a nuclear reaction), an iron core begins to form, which accumulates over time. Eventually, the temperature and pressure in the core become high enough for electrons to interact with protons in the iron nuclei to produce neutrons. In a matter of moments, this reaction is complete. The core falls and collides with the star's outer envelope, causing a massive explosion (a supernova). This continues until the neutrons exert degeneracy pressure; this creates a pulsar. In more massive stars, nothing can stop the collapse, which ends in the creation of a black hole.

METEOROID

A **meteoroid** is a small, solid fragment of material in the solar system. An enormous number of these objects are present in the system. The term meteor is used to refer to such a body when it enters the Earth's atmosphere. Interaction (friction) between meteors and the upper levels of the atmosphere cause them to break up; most disintegrate before they reach the surface. The heat associated with frictional forces causes meteors to glow, creating the phenomena of shooting stars. The meteors that are large enough to avoid complete disintegration, and can therefore travel all the way down through the atmosphere to Earth's surface, are termed meteorites. Analysis of these fragments indicates that these bodies originate from the Moon, Mars, comets, and small asteroids that cross Earth's orbital path. The forceful impacts of meteorites on Earth's surface compress, heat, and vaporize some of the materials of the meteorite as well as crustal materials, producing gases and water vapor.

ASTEROID

An **asteroid** is a small, solid planet (planetoid) that orbits the Sun. The orbital paths of most asteroids are between the orbits of Jupiter and Mars. Many of these bodies have been studied extensively and given names; those in the main belt (which tend to be carbonaceous) are classified into subgroups based on their distance from a large, named asteroid (for example, Floras, Hildas, Cybeles). **Atens** are asteroids whose orbits lie between the Earth and the Sun, and Apollos are asteroids with orbits that mimic Earth's. Asteroids may also be classified based on their composition. **C-type asteroids are similar in composition to the non-volatile elements of the sun. The sun is composed of about 74% hydrogen, 24% helium, and about 2% heavier elements**. S-type asteroids are made up of nickel-iron and iron- and magnesium-silicates; these are relatively bright. **Bright asteroids** made up exclusively of nickel-iron are classified as M-type. Observation of the relative brightness of an asteroid allows astronomers to estimate its size.

Review Video: Comets, Asteroids, and Meteoroids
Visit mometrix.com/academy and enter code: 100347

Interstellar Medium

The **interstellar**, or interplanetary, **medium** (the space between planets and stars) is populated by comets, asteroids, and meteoroids. However, particles exist in this medium on an even smaller scale. Tiny solid bodies (close to a millionth of a meter in diameter) are called **interplanetary dust**. The accumulation of this material in arctic lakes, for example, allows scientists to study it. Such analysis has revealed that these grains are most likely miniscule fragments of the **nuclei of dead comets**. They possess low density, for they are really many microscopic particles stuck together. The interplanetary dust refracts sunlight, which produces a visible (but faint) glow in parts of the sky populated by clouds of this dust. The interstellar medium also contains particle remnants of **dead stars** and **gases** (such as hydrogen molecules ionized by ultraviolet photons). **Black holes** (objects that collapse under their own gravitational forces), which trap photons, are also believed to populate the interstellar medium. Black holes are a form of dark matter.

Dark Matter

Observations of the **gravitational force** in the solar system (based on Kepler's laws) have indicated for years that there are bodies in the system that we cannot see. **Dark matter** (sometimes called missing matter) is thought to account for the unseen masses, though its exact nature is unknown. Some dark matter may simply be **ordinary celestial bodies** too small to be observed from Earth, even with technology such as high-powered telescopes. The presence of MACHOs (massive compact halo objects) has been noted through observation of distant galaxies—at certain times astronomers can discern dips in the brightness of these galaxies, thought to be caused by a large object (a MACHO) passing between Earth and the galaxy under observation. Some have postulated that dark matter is made up of **WIMPs** (weakly interacting massive particles), which do not interact with photons or other forms of electromagnetic radiation; these particles are hypothetical, because astronomers cannot detect or study them.

Review Video: Dark Matter
Visit mometrix.com/academy and enter code: 251909

Eclipses

Eclipses occur when one celestial body obscures the view of another, either partially or completely. A **solar eclipse**, or eclipse of the Sun by the Moon, happens when the Moon passes directly in front of the Sun (as observed from Earth). Alternately, a **lunar eclipse** occurs when the Moon is situated in the Earth's shadow and is therefore completely invisible. These events do not happen every month because of the differential between the orbital planes of the Moon and the Earth—the Moon's orbit is about five degrees off from the ecliptic. The Moon's orbital path is subject to the same precession that occurs in the Earth's rotational axis; this causes the occasional intersection of the orbital planes of the two bodies. Therefore, eclipses are produced by a combination of the effects of the precession of the Moon's orbit, the orbit itself, and the Earth's orbit.

Review Video: Eclipses
Visit mometrix.com/academy and enter code: 691598

Newton's Law of Gravitation

Newton's law of gravitation (sometimes referred to as the law of universal gravitation) states that the force of gravity operates as an attractive force between all bodies in the universe. Prior to Newton's formulation of this law, scientists believed that two gravitational forces were at work in the universe—that gravity operated differently on Earth than it did in space. Newton's discovery served to unify these two conceptions of gravity. This law is expressed as a mathematical formula:

$F = \frac{GMm}{D^2}$, in which F is the gravitational force, M and m are the masses of two bodies, D is the distance between them, and G is the gravitational constant ($6.67 \times 10^{-11} \frac{\text{m}^3}{\text{kg s}^2}$). The gravitational attraction between two objects, therefore, depends on the distance between them and their relative masses. Newton's law of gravitation served to clarify the mechanisms by which Kepler's laws operated. In effect, Newton proved Kepler's laws to be true through the development of this law.

Review Video: Newton's Law of Gravitation
Visit mometrix.com/academy and enter code: 709086

Characteristics of the Milky Way and Other Galaxies

Milky Way

The **Milky Way**, which houses the Earth's solar system, is a spiral galaxy. It consists of a central bulging disk, the center of which is referred to as a **nucleus**. Most of a galaxy's visible light comes from stars in this region. The disk is surrounded by a halo of stars and star clusters that spread above, next to, and beneath the nucleus. **Globular clusters** (dense, spherical clusters of ancient stars) are often found in the halo. Spiral arms of high-luminosity stars (from which this type of galaxy gets its name) fan out from the nucleus as well, with stars that are less bright in between. Interstellar dust populates the entire galaxy between celestial bodies. The entire galaxy rotates about the center. While Earth, the Sun, and its solar system are located on the disk, we are far from the center of the Milky Way. The galaxy's mass is about 1.5 trillion solar masses.

Structures of Galaxies

Elliptical galaxies are roughly spherical. Within this category, subgroups based on the degree of flattening exhibited in the galaxy's shape range from E0 (spherical) to E7 (flat). A dwarf elliptical galaxy has a spheroidal shape, with low mass and low luminosity. An S0 galaxy is similar in shape to a spiral galaxy, but lacks spiral arms. Spiral galaxies such as the Milky Way are characterized by disk-like nuclei with spiral arms. Subtypes of this category are determined by the tightness of the spiral arms and the size of the nucleus; a spiral galaxy of Sa type has a large nucleus and tightly wound arms, and an Sc-type galaxy consists of a small nucleus with open spiral arms. A barred spiral galaxy exhibits an elongated nucleus. The subtypes of barred spiral galaxies are determined like those of spiral galaxies. Some irregular galaxies (type I) display a loose spiral structure with high levels of disorganization. Other irregular galaxies (type II) can be of any shape.

Review Video: Galaxies
Visit mometrix.com/academy and enter code: 226539

Theories Relating to the Origin of the Universe

Model of the Inflationary Universe

Hubble's law states that the speed at which a galaxy appears to be moving away from the Earth is proportional to its distance from Earth. This relatively simple formula ($v = Hr$, where v is the **velocity of a receding galaxy**, r is its distance from Earth, and H is the Hubble constant) had an important implication at the time that it was developed—the universe is expanding. This fact, in turn, implies that the universe began at a **specific point** in the past. This model suggests that a random conglomeration of quarks and leptons, along with the strong force (all the forces in the universe unified as one), existed in the very dense, very hot, early universe. When the universe was a certain age (about 10–35 seconds old), the strong force separated out from the mass. This enabled the rapid expansion of the particles that formed the universe.

Big Bang Theory

The **theory of the big bang** expands upon the model of the **inflationary universe**. This theory hypothesizes that the early universe consisted of elementary particles, high energy density and high levels of pressure and heat. This single mass experienced a **phase change** (similar to that of freezing water) when it cooled and expanded. This transition caused the early universe to expand exponentially; this period of growth is called **cosmic inflation**. As it continued to grow, the temperature continued to fall. At some point, **baryogenesis** (an unknown process in which quarks and gluons become baryons, such as protons and neutrons) occurred, somehow creating the distinction between matter and antimatter. As the universe continued to cool, the **elementary forces** reached their present form, and **elementary particles** engaged in big bang **nucleosynthesis** (a process that produced helium and deuterium nuclei). **Gravity** became the predominant force governing interactions between particles; this enabled increasing accretion of particles of matter, which eventually formed the universal constituents as we recognize them today.

Chapter Quiz

Ready to see how well you retained what you just read? Scan the QR code to go directly to the chapter quiz interface for this study guide. If you're using a computer, simply visit the online resources page at **mometrix.com/resources719/ssregearthsci** and click the Chapter Quizzes link.

Regents Practice Test #1

Want to take this practice test in an online interactive format?
Check out the online resources page, which includes interactive practice questions and much more: **mometrix.com/resources719/ssregearthsci**

1. Which of the following statements correctly describes a similarity or difference between rocks and minerals?

a. Minerals may contain traces of organic compounds, while rocks do not.
b. Rocks are classified by their formation and the minerals they contain, while minerals are classified by their chemical composition and physical properties.
c. Both rocks and minerals can be polymorphs.
d. Both rocks and minerals may contain mineraloids.

2. All of the following are branches of petrology EXCEPT:

a. Metamorphic petrology
b. Igneous petrology
c. Mineralogical petrology
d. Sedimentary petrology

3. Which of these minerals would have the lowest score on the Mohs scale?

a. Gypsum
b. Fluorite
c. Talc
d. Diamond

4. Galena, pyrite, and magnetite are examples of minerals with which of the following types of luster?

a. Pearly
b. Greasy
c. Adamantine
d. Metallic

5. According to the Dana classification system, minerals that contain the anion SO_4^{2-} are part of which chemical class?

a. Sulfate
b. Sulfite
c. Halide
d. Phosphate

6. The lithification process results in the formation of which of the following types of rocks?

a. Sedimentary
b. Intrusive igneous
c. Extrusive igneous
d. Metamorphic

7. Which of the following factors directly contributes to soil erosion?

a. Air pollution from cars and factories
b. Use of pesticides
c. Deforestation and overgrazing
d. Water pollution caused by excess sedimentation

8. Which of the following is NOT an example of chemical weathering of rocks?

a. Highly acidic rainwater causes dissolution of rocks.
b. Anhydrous minerals within rocks absorb water causing them to enlarge and create fractures within the rocks.
c. Salt water penetrates fractures in rocks and leaves behind salt crystals that cause fractures.
d. Iron molecules in rocks react with atmospheric oxygen, which causes oxidation.

9. Which of the following is required for the process of diagenesis (also called lithification)?

a. Magma
b. Water
c. Wind
d. Sulfur

10. Leaching in the "A" soil horizon results from:

a. The accumulation of cations in the "B" horizon.
b. The accumulation of cations in the "O" horizon.
c. Contact with acid solutions generated in the "O" horizon.
d. Contact with acid solutions generated in the "B" horizon.

11. Metamorphic rock is produced when which of the following undergoes profound changes as a result of exposure to intense pressure and heat?

a. A batholith
b. A protolith
c. A subduction zone
d. A volcano

12. When metamorphic rock is stressed unevenly during recrystallization, it can result in:

a. Foliation
b. Contact metamorphism
c. Regional metamorphism
d. Extrusion

13. When two tectonic plates are moving laterally in opposing directions, this is called a:

a. Transformational boundary.
b. Compressional boundary.
c. Oppositional boundary.
d. Lateral boundary.

14. The most recently formed parts of the Earth's crust can be found at:

a. Subduction zones
b. Compressional boundaries
c. Extensional boundaries
d. Mid-ocean ridges

15. Which of the following events immediately precedes a volcanic eruption?

a. A batholith forms beneath the Earth's surface.
b. Magma fills vertical and horizontal fractures in the Earth's crust, creating sills and dikes.
c. An oceanic plate is subducted by a continental plate.
d. A dike reaches the Earth's surface and a plume passes through it.

16. Island chains like the Hawaiian or Midway Islands are created when:

a. Tectonic plates move apart and magma rises to the surface.
b. The subduction process creates magma, which rises above the ocean's surface to form islands.
c. Underwater earthquakes produce mountains that protrude above the water's surface.
d. A tectonic plate gradually moves over a fixed plume of magma that rises from the mantle.

17. The mountain below has the oldest rock in its core and the youngest rock in its outer layers. Which of the following terms best describes the mountain?

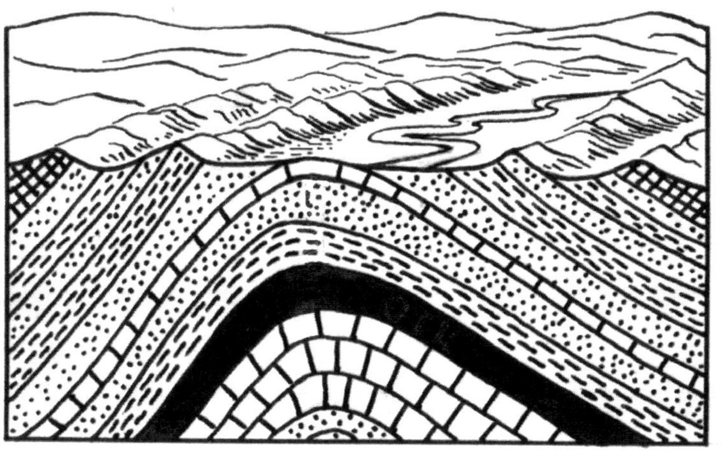

a. Syncline
b. Anticline
c. Fault-block
d. Graben

18. Which of the following is thought to be a direct result of the Dynamo Effect?

a. The motion of tectonic plates over the mantle
b. The heating of the Earth's atmosphere
c. The production of the Earth's magnetic field
d. None of the above

19. In 1912, Alfred Wegener proposed that:

a. The Earth's magnetic poles have reversed several times throughout history.
b. Tectonic plates move because of convection currents in the mantle.
c. Mountains are formed by tectonic plates pushing against one another.
d. The continents once formed a single land mass, but have since drifted apart.

20. An earthquake with a Richter magnitude of 1.5 can be expected to have which of the following effects on an urban area with high standards for building construction?

a. The earthquake will probably not be felt, and will not cause damage.
b. There may be slight damage to well-constructed buildings over a small area.
c. There will be serious damage to well-constructed buildings over a large area.
d. There will be catastrophic damage and many people will be injured.

21. Which of the following statements correctly describes the relationship between temperature and density in water?

a. As the temperature of liquid water decreases, density decreases monotonically.
b. As the temperature of frozen water (ice) increases, density decreases monotonically.
c. Water in the solid state generally has a higher density than water in the liquid state.
d. Water in the liquid state generally has a higher density than water in the solid state.

22. Water that evaporates from oceans can precipitate over land due to the process of:

a. Transpiration.
b. Advection.
c. Sublimation.
d. Interception.

23. What is the point of a phase diagram where a substance can exist as a solid, a liquid, and a gas?

a. Isothermal point
b. Isobaric point
c. Triple point
d. Critical point

24. The majority of the solar energy that reaches Earth is absorbed by:

a. Glaciers
b. Landmasses
c. Oceans
d. The Earth's atmosphere

25. According to the Köppen Climate Classification System, regions with continental climates are most commonly found:

a. In the interior regions of large landmasses.
b. Near the equator.
c. Near the Earth's poles.
d. In places with high temperatures year-round.

26. Which of the following is a true statement about the Earth's oceans?

a. Oceans comprise about 50% of the Earth's surface.
b. The deepest point in the ocean is about 6,000 meters below sea level.
c. The ocean is divided geographically into four areas: the Atlantic, Pacific, Mediterranean, and Indian.
d. The ocean's salinity is usually between 34 and 35 parts per thousand, or 200 parts per million.

27. Approximately 96.5% of seawater is composed of:

a. Hydrogen and sodium.
b. Hydrogen and oxygen.
c. Oxygen and sodium.
d. Chlorine and sodium.

28. The Coriolis effect in the Earth's oceans is caused by:

a. The Earth's rotation.
b. The Earth's magnetic field.
c. Variations in the density of seawater.
d. The Gulf Stream.

29. Thermohaline circulation is caused by:

a. Temperature differences between seawater only.
b. Salinity differences between seawater only.
c. Variations in seawater density caused by both temperature and salinity differences.
d. None of the above

30. The frequency of ocean waves is measured by:

a. The vertical distance between a wave's crest and trough
b. The horizontal distance between the crests of two subsequent waves
c. The time between two subsequent wave crests
d. The number of wave crests that pass a given point each second

31. The Cretaceous-Tertiary event, during which non-avian dinosaurs became extinct, occurred approximately how long ago?

a. 10,000 years ago
b. 15.5 million years ago
c. 38 million years ago
d. 65.5 million years ago

32. In the field of geology, the term "uniformitarianism" refers to the belief that:

a. Catastrophic events like mass extinctions are the main forces that have shaped the Earth.
b. The Earth's crust has not undergone any dramatic changes since its formation.
c. The natural forces that shape the Earth have remained relatively constant over geologic time.
d. The Earth's stratigraphy is more or less uniform at any given geographic location.

33. Which of the following is an example of an absolute age?

a. A fossil is 37 million years old.
b. A rock is less than 100,000 years old.
c. An organic artifact is between 5,000 and 10,000 years old.
d. All of the above

34. Which of the following correctly lists the periods that make up the Mesozoic era, from earliest to most recent?

a. Jurassic, Triassic, Cretaceous
b. Permian, Triassic, Jurassic
c. Triassic, Jurassic, Cretaceous
d. Triassic, Jurassic, Permian

35. According to current theories, the Earth was formed approximately how long ago?

a. 50 million years ago
b. 1.25 billion years ago
c. 4.5 billion years ago
d. 15 billion years ago

36. Which of the following life forms appeared first on Earth?

a. Eukaryotes
b. Arthropods
c. Prokaryotes
d. Amphibians

37. Which of the following is considered observational evidence in support of the Big Bang Theory?

a. Expansion in the redshifts of galaxies
b. Measurements of cosmic microwave background radiation
c. Measurements of the distribution of quasars and galaxies
d. All of the above

38. Redshift is observed when:

a. A light-emitting object moves away from an observer.
b. A star begins to decrease the amount of light it emits.
c. A light-emitting object moves toward an observer.
d. A magnetic field bends observed light.

39. Which of the following statements about galaxies is true?

a. Galaxies are the only structures in the universe that do not contain dark matter.
b. Galaxies are gravitationally bound, meaning structures within the galaxy orbit around its center.
c. Galaxies typically contain over one trillion stars.
d. Galaxies are composed of clusters and superclusters.

40. The Hertzsprung-Russell (H-R) Diagram is used primarily to:

a. Determine a star's age by comparing its temperature and luminosity.
b. Measure a star's size by estimating its luminosity.
c. Determine a galaxy's luminosity when its size is known.
d. Group galaxies by their morphological types.

41. The energy radiated by stars is produced by:

a. Neutronicity.
b. Nuclear fusion.
c. Nuclear fission.
d. Gravitational confinement.

42. Which of the following planets in our solar system is NOT a gas giant?

a. Saturn
b. Neptune
c. Venus
d. Jupiter

43. Which of the following is a proposed explanation for the formation of black holes?

a. High-energy collisions
b. Gravitational collapse
c. Accretion of matter
d. A and B

44. The atomic number of an element is defined by:

a. The total number of protons and electrons it contains.
b. The total number of electrons it contains.
c. The total number of protons it contains.
d. The total number of neutrons it contains.

45. Which of the following statements is NOT true of electrons?

a. They comprise only a tiny fraction of an atom's mass.
b. They are arranged in levels, and usually occupy the lowest energy level possible.
c. They are negatively charged.
d. They have a substructure that includes a nucleus.

46. The state of matter in which atoms have the strongest bond is:

a. Plasma.
b. Liquid.
c. Solid.
d. Gas.

47. The formula for calculating kinetic energy is:

a. $\frac{1}{2} mv^2$.
b. $\frac{1}{2} mv$.
c. mgh.
d. mgv.

48. James Hutton is best known for:

a. Establishing the first observable evidence for the Big Bang Theory.
b. Suggesting the Third Law of Thermodynamics.
c. Proposing the theory of uniformitarianism.
d. Introducing the Law of Superposition.

49. A calorimeter is used to measure changes in:

a. Heat.
b. Mass.
c. Weight.
d. Volume.

50. Which of the following can be inferred based on the results of the regression analysis shown in the following figure?

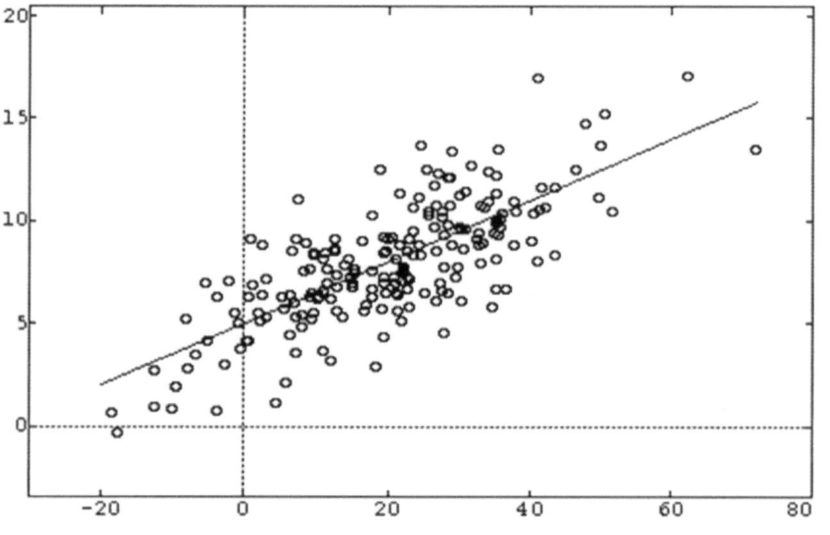

a. A change in the independent variable causes a change in the dependent variable.
b. A change in the dependent variable causes a change in the independent variable.
c. There is a weak positive correlation between the two variables.
d. There is a weak negative correlation between the two variables.

Answer Key and Explanations for Test #1

1. B: It is true that rocks are classified by their formation and the minerals they contain, while minerals are classified by their chemical composition and physical properties. Answer A is incorrect because rocks may contain traces of organic compounds. Answers C and D are incorrect because only minerals can be polymorphs and only rocks contain mineraloids.

2. C: Mineralogical petrology is not a branch of petrology. Petrologists study the various categories of rocks, including metamorphic, igneous, and sedimentary. Some petrologists, called experimental petrologists, also study changes in the geochemistry of materials that are exposed to extreme temperatures and pressures. Minerals are studied by mineralogists, not petrologists.

3. C: On the Mohs scale of mineral hardness, talc has the lowest possible score (a one). Diamond is a ten, which is the highest possible score, and gypsum and fluorite have a score of two and four, respectively. Minerals can always scratch minerals that have a Mohs score lower than their own.

4. D: Galena, pyrite, and magnetite are examples of minerals with a metallic luster. Opal is an example of a mineral with a greasy luster, and diamonds have an adamantine luster. Muscovite and stilbite are examples of minerals with a pearly luster. Other types of luster include dull, silky, waxy, and sub-metallic.

5. A: According to the Dana system, minerals that contain the anion SO42- are part of the sulfate class. Sulfate minerals are typically formed in environments where high salinity water evaporates. Gypsum is an example of a mineral that belongs to the sulfate class.

6. A: The lithification process results in the formation of sedimentary rocks. During lithification, existing rock is compacted and liquid is squeezed from its pores. Eventually, the rock is cemented together, resulting in sedimentary rock.

7. C: Overgrazing and deforestation directly contribute to soil erosion by destroying the natural ground cover that normally prevents soil from being washed and blown away. These activities can ultimately result in desertification, which renders land unsuitable for agriculture.

8. C: When salt water penetrates fractures in rocks and leaves behind salt crystals that cause the rock to fracture, it is considered physical rather than chemical weathering. Chemical weathering involves changes in the molecules that make up the rocks, while physical weathering occurs when external factors act on the rock without changing its chemical composition in any way.

9. B: Water is a key element in the lithification of sedimentary rock. After it is squeezed from the compressed material, it forms a chemical cement that holds the sedimentary rock in place. This cementation process is followed by recrystallization of the rock when equilibrium is reached.

10. C: Leaching in the "A" soil horizon results from contact with acid solutions generated in the "O" horizon, which is the uppermost organic layer of soil. Cations that are leached in the "A" soil horizon accumulate in the "B" soil horizon below.

11. B: Metamorphic rock is produced when a protolith undergoes profound changes after being exposed to extreme heat and pressure. A protolith is any rock that is transformed through this process. The original rock may be sedimentary, igneous, or metamorphic. The extreme heat and pressure that serve as the catalyst for this transformation may be produced by the intrusion of magma or tectonic activity, among other factors.

12. A: When metamorphic rock is stressed unevenly during recrystallization, it can result in foliation. Foliation is characterized by banded rock, and it occurs when certain types of minerals are reoriented during recrystallization due to uneven shortening or compression of the rock.

13. A: When two tectonic plates are moving laterally in opposing directions, this is called a transform boundary. When there is friction at transform boundaries and pressure builds up, it can result in shallow earthquakes (usually at a depth of less than 25 meters). California's San Andreas Fault is an example of a transform boundary.

14. D: The most recently formed parts of the Earth's crust can be found at mid-ocean ridges. New crust forms here when magma erupts from these ridges and pushes preexisting crust horizontally towards the continental plates. Such ridges include the Mid-Atlantic Ridge and the East Pacific Rise.

15. D: A volcano occurs when a dike (a vertical fracture in the Earth's crust that fills with magma) reaches the Earth's surface and a plume (a spurt of magma) passes through it. Batholiths are large masses of igneous rock that form beneath the Earth's surface, and a sill is a horizontal fracture in the Earth's crust that fills with magma. When an oceanic plate is subducted by a continental plate, it results in the formation of mountain ranges.

16. D: Island chains like the Hawaiian or Midway Islands are created when a tectonic plate gradually moves over a fixed plume of magma that rises from the mantle. When this plume erupts through the Earth's crust, a volcano that rises above the water's surface is formed, which creates an island. The tectonic plate gradually shifts so that the next time the fixed plume erupts, it affects a different point on the plate. This creates another volcanic island near the first one.

17. B: Since the mountain in the figure has the oldest rock in its core and the youngest rock in its outer layers, it is best described as an anticline. Any mountain that results from a crustal fold and has an upward, convex shape is called an antiform. Mountains in which the rocks are progressively older from the outer layers to the core are anticlines. Synclines have downward, or concave, folds, and fault-block mountains result when faults in continental crust cause certain sections to lift or tilt. Grabens are a formation associated with fault-block mountains.

18. C: The Earth's magnetic field is thought to be produced by the Dynamo Effect. According to this theory, the Earth's rotation combined with the convection of metals within the Earth's core produce electric currents. When these currents flow through an existing magnetic field in the core, this produces a secondary magnetic field which reinforces the primary field and creates a self-sustaining dynamo.

19. D: In 1912, Alfred Wegener proposed that the continents once formed a single land mass called Pangaea, but have since drifted apart. Theories about the Earth's magnetic fields and plate tectonics did not emerge until years later. Once they did, they helped produce evidence to support Wegener's theory.

20. A: An earthquake with a Richter magnitude of 1.5 will probably not be felt, and will not cause any damage. Earthquakes with magnitudes of less than 2.0 are usually not felt, and those with magnitudes of less than 5.0 typically do not seriously damage well-constructed buildings. Earthquakes with magnitudes of 6.0 or greater can cause damage to even well-constructed buildings.

21. D: Water in the liquid state generally has a higher density than water in the solid state (ice). Unlike most other substances, which become progressively denser as they grow colder, water's density only increases until it reaches a maximum density around 4 °C, after which it begins to decrease as the temperature drops further.

22. B: Water that evaporates from oceans can precipitate over land due to the process of advection. Water vapor is less dense than air, and this difference in density produces convection currents that move the vapor, allowing it to condense and precipitate over land masses.

23. C: A triple point on a phase diagram indicates a precise temperature and pressure where a substance can simultaneously exist as a solid, a liquid, and a gas. Isothermal means constant temperature and would refer to a vertical line rather than a point. Isobaric means constant pressure and would refer to a horizontal line rather than a point. The critical point indicates a particular temperature and pressure beyond which the substance is neither a liquid nor a gas, but a supercritical fluid.

24. C: The majority of the solar energy that reaches Earth is absorbed by the oceans, which make up 71 percent of the Earth's surface. Because of water's high specific heat capacity, oceans can absorb and store large quantities of heat, thus preventing drastic increases in the overall atmospheric temperature.

25. A: According to the Köppen Climate Classification System, regions with continental climates are most commonly found in the interior regions of large landmasses. The continental climate is characterized by low levels of precipitation and large seasonal temperature variations.

26. D: It is true that the ocean's salinity is usually between 34 and 35 parts per thousand, or 200 parts per million. Oceans comprise about 70.8% of the Earth's surface, and the ocean's deepest point is over 10,000 meters below sea level. The Mediterranean is considered a sea, not an ocean.

27. B: Approximately 96.5% of seawater is composed of hydrogen and oxygen. Although seawater does contain sodium, chlorine, magnesium, sulfur, and other dissolved solids, its primary components are the same substances that make up fresh water.

28. A: The appearance of the Coriolis effect in the Earth's oceans is caused by the Earth's rotation. The Coriolis effect results when free objects such as water move over a rotating surface such as the Earth. As water moves from the poles towards the equator, it curves slightly westward, while water moving in the opposite direction (from the equator towards the poles) moves slightly eastward.

29. C: Thermohaline circulation is caused by variations in seawater density caused by both temperature and salinity differences. This process, which affects subsurface ocean currents, contributes to the mixing of seawater and accounts for the relative uniformity of the water's physical and chemical properties.

30. D: The frequency of ocean waves is measured by the number of wave crests that pass a given point each second. The crest of a wave is its highest point, and the trough is its lowest point. The horizontal distance between two subsequent crests is called wavelength, and the height is the vertical distance between a single wave's trough and crest.

31. D: The Cretaceous-Tertiary event, during which non-avian dinosaurs became extinct, occurred approximately 65.5 million years ago, during the Mesozoic era. It is the most recent of the five major extinction events that have occurred throughout the Earth's history.

32. C: In the field of geology, the term "uniformitarianism" refers to the belief that the natural forces, laws, and processes that shape the Earth have remained relatively constant over geologic time. This belief contradicts catastrophism, which maintains that dramatic events have been the primary forces involved in shaping the Earth.

33. A: When a fossil is determined to be 37 million years old, this is an example of an absolute age. Absolute dating, which can be accomplished through the use of radiometric techniques, establishes precise ages for materials, while stratigraphic techniques only produce relative dates. Relative dating can establish approximate ages for rocks and fossils based on clues in the surrounding rock, but it cannot be used to determine absolute age.

34. C: The Mesozoic era is composed of the Triassic, Jurassic, and Cretaceous periods. It was preceded by the Paleozoic era, of which the Permian is the last period. The Triassic period ended about 200 million years ago, and was followed by the Jurassic period. The Jurassic period gave way to the Cretaceous period just under 150 million years ago.

35. C: According to current theories, the Earth was formed approximately 4.5 billion years ago. This date has been established through the use of radiometric dating performed on meteorite fossils.

36. C: Prokaryotes, or simple cells that lack a nucleus, appeared on Earth approximately 3.8 billion years ago. Eukaryotes, or complex cells, emerged 2 billion years ago, and arthropods developed about 570 million years ago. Amphibians emerged approximately 360 million years ago.

37. D: Expansion in the redshifts of galaxies, measurements of cosmic microwave background radiation, and measurements of the distribution of quasars and galaxies are all considered observational evidence in support of the Big Bang Theory. The abundance of certain "primordial elements" is also consistent with the theory.

38. A: Redshift is observed when a light-emitting object moves away from an observer. The observation of cosmological redshift supports the notion that the universe is expanding and the distance between Earth and distant galaxies is increasing. Redshift is an increase in the wavelength of light that appears visually as a movement toward the "red" end of the spectrum.

39. B: It is true that galaxies are gravitationally bound, so that structures within them orbit around the center. Galaxies do contain dark matter, and only the largest "giant" galaxies contain over one trillion stars. The smallest "dwarf" galaxies contain as few as 10 million stars. Clusters and superclusters are composed of many galaxies.

40. A: The Hertzsprung-Russell (H-R) Diagram is used primarily to determine a star's age by comparing its temperature and luminosity. These two variables are plotted, and a given star's values can be compared to those of other stars to estimate its age and evolutionary stage. Stars on the Main Sequence of the diagram have roughly proportional luminosity and temperature values, while white dwarf stars have low luminosity relative to their temperature. Some giant stars have low temperatures relative to their luminosity.

41. B: The energy radiated by stars is produced by nuclear fusion. This is the process whereby the nuclei of individual atoms bind together to form heavier elements and release energy outward. By the time this energy, which is created in the star's core, reaches the outer walls of the star, it exists in the form of light.

42. C: Venus is not a gas giant. The four gas giants are Jupiter, Saturn, Uranus, and Neptune. While these gas giants are larger than Earth and are composed mostly of gases, Venus is a terrestrial planet that is comparable in size to the Earth.

43. D: Gravitational collapse and high-energy collisions are both proposed explanations for the formation of black holes. Gravitational collapse occurs when the outward pressure exerted by an object is too weak to resist that object's own gravity. Collisions that produce conditions of sufficient density could also, in theory, create black holes. The accretion of matter is considered observational evidence for the existence of black holes.

44. C: The atomic number of an element is defined by the total number of protons it contains, and elements are arranged on the periodic table by atomic number. The atomic mass of an element is the sum total of its protons and neutrons, averaged over all of its isotopes.

45. D: Electrons are elementary particles with no known components, so it is not true that they have a nucleus. Electrons are negatively charged, and they are arranged in levels. Electrons gravitate toward the lowest energy level possible, and they have very little mass (roughly 1/1836 of the mass of a proton).

46. C: The state of matter in which atoms have the strongest bond is the solid state. Matter, which is defined as any substance that has mass and occupies space, can exist as a solid, liquid, gas, or plasma. The atoms or molecules that form solids possess the strongest bonds, while those that form plasma possess the weakest bonds.

47. A: The formula for calculating kinetic energy is $\frac{1}{2}mv^2$, where *m*=mass and *v*=velocity. Kinetic energy is defined as the energy of an object in motion. Potential energy, or stored energy, is measured using the formula *mgh*, where *m*=mass, *g*=gravity, and *h*=height.

48. C: James Hutton is best known for proposing the theory of uniformitarianism. This geological theory, which is essentially the opposite of catastrophism, suggests that the laws and forces acting on the Earth have remained basically the same since the beginning of geologic time.

49. A: A calorimeter is used to measure changes in heat. This instrument uses a thermometer to measure the amount of energy necessary to increase the temperature of water.

50. C: The results of the regression analysis show that there is a weak positive correlation between the two variables, as evidenced by the fact that data points with higher values for the independent variable (x-axis) also have higher corresponding values for the dependent variable (y-axis). However, correlation does not equal causation, and it cannot be established that a change in the independent variable causes a corresponding change in the dependent variable without additional information.

Regents Practice Test #2

1. Which of the following is the best description of mineraloids?

a. Mineraloids are organic compounds found in rocks.
b. Mineraloids are inorganic solids containing two or more minerals with different crystalline structures.
c. Mineraloids are inorganic solids containing one or more minerals with the same crystalline structure.
d. Mineraloids are similar to minerals, but they lack a crystalline structure.

2. Which of the following is NOT one of the five major physical properties of minerals?

a. Chemical composition
b. Hardness
c. Luster
d. Streak

3. A mineral's true color is observed by:

a. Conducting a streak test on white paper.
b. Conducting a streak test on unglazed porcelain tile.
c. Inspecting the mineral's outer surface.
d. Shining a light on the mineral to inspect its luster.

4. According to the Dana classification system, gold, silver, and copper belong to which class?

a. Organic
b. Elemental
c. Oxide
d. Sulfide

5. Minerals that form on the sea floor from discarded shells are most likely part of which chemical class?

a. Sulfate
b. Organic
c. Carbonate
d. Silicate

6. Which of the following types of igneous rock solidifies deepest beneath the Earth's surface?

a. Hypabyssal
b. Plutonic
c. Volcanic
d. Detrital

7. Physical weathering of rocks can be caused by all of the following EXCEPT:

a. The freezing and thawing of water on the surface of rocks
b. Changes in temperature
c. Oxidation
d. Changes in pressure due to the removal of overlying rocks

8. Which of the following lists places several phases of the sedimentary cycle in the correct order?

a. Erosion, weathering, transportation, deposition
b. Weathering, erosion, deposition, transportation
c. Weathering, deposition, erosion, transportation
d. Weathering, erosion, transportation, deposition

9. Nondetrital sedimentary rock is produced by:

a. Chemical precipitation.
b. Cooling of magma just below the Earth's surface.
c. Physical weathering processes.
d. Weathering of igneous rock.

10. Which of the following statements is true of Rocks (such as olivine) that are found at the top of Bowen's reaction series?

a. They are classified as metamorphic.
b. They weather more quickly than rocks found lower in the series.
c. They crystallize at lower temperatures than rocks found at the bottom of the series.
d. None of the above

11. All of the following are examples of metamorphic rocks EXCEPT:

a. Granite
b. Quartzite
c. Slate
d. Marble

12. Which of the following statements correctly describes a distinction between regional and contact metamorphism?

a. Regional metamorphism results from intense heat, while contact metamorphism is caused by extreme pressure.
b. Regional metamorphism results from extreme pressure, while contact metamorphism is caused by intense heat.
c. Regional metamorphism occurs when magma is injected into surrounding rock, while contact metamorphism occurs when a large area of rock is subjected to intense heat and pressure.
d. Regional metamorphism occurs when a large area of rock is subjected to intense heat and pressure, while contact metamorphism occurs when magma is injected into surrounding rock.

13. Which of the following statements correctly describes a difference between the lithosphere and the asthenosphere?

a. The asthenosphere is composed of atmospheric gas, while the lithosphere is composed of liquids and solids.
b. The asthenosphere is hotter and more fluid than the lithosphere.
c. The lithosphere is hotter and has a different chemical composition than the asthenosphere.
d. Heat is transferred through conduction in the asthenosphere, while it is transferred through convection in the lithosphere.

14. When an earthquake occurs, the shaking that is observed results directly from:

a. Static deformation.
b. Seismic waves.
c. Compression waves.
d. Continental drift.

15. Cinder cone volcanoes are created by:

a. A series of explosive eruptions.
b. Gradual eruptions over time.
c. A combination of both explosive and gradual eruptions over time.
d. None of the above

16. Which of the following is true of a volcano that is thought to be dormant?

a. It will probably never erupt again, and it is quite safe for people to live near its base.
b. It is expected to erupt some time again in the future, but danger is not imminent.
c. It is expected to erupt soon, and evacuation should be commenced.
d. It is a shield volcano that is erupting, but people living near the volcano should not expect their lives to be significantly disrupted.

17. When fault-block mountains like those in the Western United States are formed, sections that are lifted by tensional forces are called:

a. Antiforms.
b. Faces.
c. Horsts.
d. Rifts.

18. The Earth's magnetic field protects it from:

a. Excess heat from the Sun
b. Radio waves from black holes
c. Solar wind
d. Impacts from space debris

19. The Richter scale determines the magnitude of an earthquake by:

a. Comparing its destructiveness to that of other earthquakes.
b. Measuring the amount of seismic energy it releases.
c. Ascertaining the farthest distance from the epicenter at which the earthquake can be felt.
d. Measuring the depth of the earthquake.

20. The process that causes lithospheric plates to move over the surface of the mantle is called:

a. Conduction
b. Convection
c. Tension
d. Subduction

21. Ammonia has a specific heat capacity greater than that of water. This means that:

a. Water vaporizes at a higher temperature than ammonia.
b. It takes more energy to increase the temperature of ammonia than it does to increase the temperature of water.
c. Water is always denser than ammonia.
d. Water is only denser than ammonia at higher temperatures.

22. Water is likely to have the shortest residence time in which of the following types of reservoirs?

a. A glacier
b. A lake
c. A river
d. The atmosphere

23. The main human-caused reason for "dead zones" in portions of oceans and lakes that normally host abundant aquatic life is:

a. Evaporation.
b. Invasive species.
c. Use of chemical fertilizers.
d. Global warming.

24. The majority of weather phenomena occur in which part of the Earth's atmosphere?

a. Troposphere
b. Stratosphere
c. Hydrosphere
d. Ionosphere

25. Tropical climate zones are characterized by:

a. Extreme temperature variations between night and day.
b. Extreme temperature variations between seasons.
c. Frequent rainfall.
d. All of the above

26. A guyot is defined as:

a. Any undersea mountain more than 1,000 meters high
b. A seamount with a flattened top
c. An undersea mountain chain
d. A trough in the ocean floor

27. Which of the following statements correctly describes a difference between surface and subsurface ocean currents?

a. Subsurface currents are caused only by temperature variations, while surface currents are caused by changes in air pressure.
b. Subsurface currents are caused by temperature and density variations, while surface currents are caused by changes in air pressure.
c. Subsurface currents are caused by temperature and density variations, while surface currents are caused by wind.
d. Surface currents are caused by changes in air temperature, while subsurface currents are caused by changes in water temperature.

28. Which of the following statements correctly describes an effect of the Gulf Stream?

a. It increases humidity along North America's west coast.
b. It makes the climate of South America colder.
c. It makes the climate of Northern Europe warmer.
d. It makes the climate of the Caribbean milder and less humid.

29. When cold, nutrient-rich water is allowed to rise to the surface because winds parallel to a landmass's coast blow the surface water towards the open sea, this is called:

a. Ekman transport.
b. The Coriolis effect.
c. Upwelling.
d. Downwelling.

30. When the accumulation of snow and ice exceeds ablation, which of the following occurs as a direct result?

a. An iceberg breaks free from a glacier.
b. A glacier gradually forms.
c. A glacier slowly erodes.
d. A lake forms within a glacier.

31. Which of the following techniques is NOT a radiometric dating process?

a. Potassium-argon dating
b. Stratigraphic dating
c. Uranium-lead dating
d. Chlorine-36 dating

32. In the field of stratigraphy, the relative ages of rocks may be determined by examining which of the following types of evidence?

a. The dates the rocks were formed and the ages of fossils deposited within the rocks
b. Evidence of changes in detrital remanent magnetism when the rock was deposited
c. The vertical layering pattern of the rock
d. All of the above

33. In geochronology, which of the following is the longest time period?

a. An epoch
b. An era
c. An eon
d. An age

34. In his work, *The Origin of Life*, Alexander Oparin argued that:

a. Life arose spontaneously from other decaying organic matter.
b. Life originated in deep-sea vents.
c. Life arose on Earth through a "primordial soup" that is no longer possible because of atmospheric oxygen.
d. Life emerged as part of an autocatalytic network.

35. The most severe mass extinction event in Earth's history was the:

a. Cretaceous-Tertiary Event.
b. Permian-Triassic Event.
c. Ordovician-Silurian Event.
d. Late Devonian Event.

36. The Cambrian Explosion is best described as:

a. A great migration of flora and fauna between North and South America that vastly increased biodiversity on both continents.
b. The emergence of multicellular life about one billion years ago.
c. The increase in the pace of evolution ushered in by the emergence of sexual reproduction about 1.2 billion years ago.
d. The dramatic increase in biodiversity that began about 530 million years ago and resulted in the emergence of complex animals over a period of millions of years.

37. The Cosmological Principle is best described as:

a. An assumption that cannot be tested empirically because it has no observable implications.
b. A scientific hypothesis that has been repeatedly validated in empirical tests.
c. A working assumption that has testable structural consequences.
d. A law of physics that defies empirical testing.

38. Which of the following statements best describes the physical structure of the universe?

a. Galaxies are the largest structures in the universe, and they are distributed evenly throughout space.
b. Superclusters are the largest structures in the universe, and they are distributed evenly throughout space.
c. Superclusters are the largest structures in the universe, and they are unevenly distributed so that large voids exist in space.
d. Filaments are the largest structures in the universe, and they surround large, bubble-like voids.

39. The structure of the Milky Way galaxy is best described as:

a. Spiral.
b. Starburst.
c. Elliptical.
d. Irregular.

40. The distance from the Earth to the Sun is equal to one:

a. Astronomical unit.
b. Light year.
c. Parsec.
d. Arcsecond.

41. The stream of charged particles that escape the Sun's gravitational pull is best described by which of the following terms?

a. Solar wind
b. Solar flare
c. Solar radiation
d. Sunspots

42. The asteroid belt in our solar system is located between:

a. Earth and Mars.
b. Neptune and Pluto.
c. Uranus and Saturn.
d. Mars and Jupiter.

43. A total solar eclipse can be observed only by viewers located:

a. Within the penumbra but outside of the umbra.
b. Within the umbra.
c. Within either the umbra or the penumbra.
d. Outside of the Moon's penumbra.

44. Which of the following statements best describes the main distinction between the isotopes carbon-12 and carbon-13?

a. They have different atomic numbers.
b. They have different mass numbers.
c. They have experienced different degrees of radioactive decay.
d. A and B

45. Chemical compounds are formed when:

a. Valence electrons from atoms of two different elements are shared or transferred.
b. Valence electrons from multiple atoms of a single element are shared or transferred.
c. The nuclei of two atoms are joined together.
d. The nucleus of an atom is split.

46. Which of the following statements is true of a closed thermodynamic system?

a. It cannot exchange heat, work, or matter with its surrounding environment.
b. It can exchange heat and work, but not matter, with its surrounding environment.
c. It can exchange heat, but not work or matter, with its surrounding environment.
d. It can exchange matter, but not heat or work, with its surrounding environment.

47. Which law of classical thermodynamics states that energy can neither be created nor destroyed?

a. Zeroth
b. First
c. Second
d. Third

48. Which of the following is the correct formula for converting Fahrenheit to Celsius?

a. $C = 5/9\ (F - 32)$
b. $C = 9/5\ (F - 32)$
c. $C = 5/9\ (F + 32)$
d. None of the above

49. Commercial nuclear reactors generate electricity through the process of:

a. Nuclear fission.
b. Nuclear fusion.
c. Nuclear depletion.
d. Radioactive decay.

50. Random error could be caused by which of the following problems?

a. Imperfectly calibrated equipment
b. Extraneous disturbances that cannot be controlled
c. Consistent human error in the use of lab equipment
d. Failure to account for a specific variable

Answer Key and Explanations for Test #2

1. D: Mineraloids can be defined as substances that resemble minerals but lack a crystalline structure. They are typically found in rocks. Inorganic solids containing two or more minerals with different crystalline structures are known as polymorphs.

2. A: Chemical composition is not one of the physical properties used to classify minerals. The five major physical properties used to classify minerals are luster, hardness, cleavage, streak, and form. There is a separate classification system based on the chemical composition of minerals.

3. B: A mineral's true color is observed by conducting a streak test on unglazed porcelain tile. Paper is not appropriate for a streak test because it does not have the correct physical properties. External observation (inspecting the mineral's outer surface) is not sufficient to establish true color since streak tests sometimes reveal a color that is different from the substance's external hue. Finally, the luster test is not used to determine color.

4. B: According to the Dana classification system, gold, silver, and copper belong to the elemental class. Members of the oxide class include chromite and magnetite, and hydrocarbons and acetates are members of the organic class. Sulfide minerals include pyrite and galena.

5. C: Minerals that form on the sea floor from discarded shells are most likely part of the carbonate class. Minerals that form in karst regions and evaporitic settings may also be carbonates. Examples of minerals in the carbonate class include aragonite, dolomite, calcite, and siderite.

6. B: Plutonic, or intrusive, rock forms deep beneath the Earth's surface and cools slowly. Volcanic, or extrusive, rock solidifies at or near the surface. Hypabyssal rock forms below the Earth's surface, but not at a depth as great as plutonic rock. Detrital rock is a type of sedimentary rock.

7. C: Physical weathering of rocks can be caused by changes in temperature and pressure, as well as the freezing and thawing of water on the surfaces of rocks. Oxidation is a chemical process, not a physical one. Therefore, it is considered an example of chemical rather than physical weathering.

8. D: Weathering causes erosion, which often leads to transportation and the deposition of eroded material. After the eroded material is deposited in a new location, lithification proceeds and the sedimentary cycle begins anew.

9. A: Non-detrital sedimentary rock is produced by chemical precipitation. In contrast, detrital sedimentary rocks are comprised of pre-existing rocks, such as quartz, or weathered products of pre-existing rocks, such as clay.

10. B: Rocks (such as olivine) that are found at the top of Bowen's reaction series weather more quickly than rocks found lower in the series. This is because rocks high in the series crystallize at higher temperatures than those found lower in the series. This means they are less stable and more susceptible to weathering than rocks that crystallize at lower temperatures, such as quartz.

11. A: Quartzite, marble, and slate are all examples of metamorphic rocks, while granite is one of the most common types of igneous rocks.

12. D: Regional metamorphism occurs when a large area of rock is subjected to intense heat and pressure, while contact metamorphism occurs when magma is injected into surrounding rock, also known as country rock. When contact metamorphism occurs, the rocks closest to the hot magma undergo the greatest changes.

13. B: It is true that the asthenosphere is hotter and more fluid than the lithosphere. The asthenosphere, also called the upper mantle, is the hot, fluid layer of the Earth's mantle upon which the lithosphere, or crust, is situated. Heat is transferred within the asthenosphere through a process called convection, which sometimes causes movement in the tectonic plates that make up the lithosphere.

14. B: When an earthquake occurs, the shaking that is observed is a direct result of seismic waves. Seismic waves are powerful sound waves released when slippage between plates occurs. There are two types of seismic waves: primary, or P-waves, and secondary, or S-waves. P-waves move more quickly than S-waves, and create motion that radiates directly outward from the point of origin. S-waves produce a shearing, or side-to-side, motion.

15. A: Cinder cone volcanoes are created by a series of explosive eruptions. Gradual eruptions produce shield volcanoes, and composite volcanoes are the result of a combination of gradual and explosive eruptions over time.

16. B: A volcano that is thought to be dormant is expected to erupt some time again in the future, but danger is not imminent. Dormant volcanoes are expected to erupt again in the future because they still show signs of internal volcanic activity. Extinct volcanoes are not expected to erupt again because they show no signs of activity. Active volcanoes are either erupting or about to erupt.

17. C: When fault-block mountains such as those in the Western United States are formed, sections that are lifted by tensional forces are called horsts. Blocks that are lowered in elevation are called grabens. The term "rift" refers to the entire area that is affected by the separation of a continental plate.

18. C: The Earth's magnetic field protects it from solar wind. Solar wind is a stream of highly charged radioactive particles that emanate from the Sun, and these particles are deflected by the magnetic field. The magnetic field is shaped like a bowl that covers the side of the Earth facing the Sun. It deflects most solar particles, but some are trapped in the Van Allen belt. Particularly strong bursts of solar wind allow particles to pass through this belt into the Earth's ionosphere and upper atmosphere, creating geomagnetic storms and auroras.

19. B: The Richter scale determines the magnitude of an earthquake by measuring the amount of seismic energy it releases. The formula used to calculate an earthquake's Richter magnitude takes the logarithm of the horizontal amplitude of the earthquake's seismic waves into account, and also makes adjustments for the position of the seismograph relative to the earthquake.

20. B: The process that causes lithospheric plates to move over the surface of the mantle is called convection. The liquid in the lower portion of the mantle is heated by the Earth's core and rises to the surface, pushing aside cooler liquid that is already there. This liquid cools, and is in turn pushed aside by hotter liquid that has risen from below. This cycle, called convection, creates constant movement in the mantle that contributes to the motion of the tectonic plates.

21. B: The fact that water's specific heat capacity is second only to that of ammonia means that it takes more energy to increase the temperature of ammonia than it does to increase the temperature of water. Specific heat capacity refers to the amount of energy required to increase the temperature of a substance by one degree Celsius. Ammonia has the highest specific heat capacity of all substances, and the specific heat capacity of water is the second highest.

22. D: Water is likely to have the shortest residence time in the atmosphere. Water molecules linger in the atmosphere for an estimated 9 days, while their residence time in glaciers may range from 20 to 100 years. Water molecules reside in lakes for approximately 50 to 100 years, and they stay in rivers for two to six months.

23. C: The main human-caused reason for "dead zones" in portions of oceans and lakes that normally host abundant aquatic life is the use of chemical fertilizers. These fertilizers, which are high in nitrogen and phosphorous, enter lakes and rivers in water runoff and become concentrated in certain areas. This concentration, called eutrophication, eventually depletes the water's oxygen levels and renders it incapable of supporting life.

24. A: The majority of weather phenomena occur in the Earth's troposphere. The troposphere is composed of the area roughly 8-15 kilometers above the Earth's surface. It contains the majority of the mass of Earth's atmosphere and 99 percent of its water vapor.

25. C: Tropical climate zones are characterized by frequent rainfall, especially during the monsoon season, and by moderate temperatures that vary little from season to season or between night and day. Tropical zones do experience frequent rainfall, which leads to abundant vegetation.

26. B: A guyot is defined as a seamount with a flattened top. The term "seamount" refers to any undersea volcano that is more than 1,000 meters tall. Undersea troughs are called trenches, and undersea mountain chains are called mid-ocean ridges.

27. C: It is true that subsurface currents are driven by temperature and density variations, while surface currents are driven by wind. Ocean currents affect vast quantities of seawater and strongly influence the climate of Earth's landmasses.

28. C: The Gulf Stream, which is a surface current that originates in the Gulf of Mexico and travels across the Atlantic Ocean, makes the climate of Northern Europe warmer. After traveling up the eastern coast of the US, the Gulf Stream splits into two forks. The North Atlantic Drift travels across the ocean to warm Europe, while the southern fork travels toward West Africa.

29. C: When cold, nutrient-rich water is allowed to rise to the surface because winds parallel to a landmass's coast blow the surface water towards the open sea, it is called upwelling. Upwelling brings the remains of dead sea creatures to the surface, providing food for phytoplankton. Zooplanktons consume the phytoplankton, and larger organisms consume the zooplanktons. Thus, upwelling allows marine life to thrive near coastal areas.

30. B: When the accumulation of snow and ice exceeds ablation, a glacier will gradually form. Ablation is the sloughing off of ice and snow through melting, evaporation, sublimation, and wind erosion. When snow and ice accumulate faster than ablation occurs, a glacier will form and continue to gain mass until the rate of ablation overtakes the rate of accumulation.

31. B: Stratigraphic dating is not a radiometric dating process because it does not consider the radioactive properties of materials to estimate their dates. Instead, it relies on the law of superposition to estimate relative ages by comparing the relative depths of materials.

32. D: The field of stratigraphy is divided into several subfields, each of which focuses on a unique aspect of sedimentary material and yields unique insights about the material's age. In the subfield of chronostratigraphy, a material's age is estimated by determining when it was formed or deposited. The study of the vertical layering of rock types is called lithostratigraphy, and the study of fossil ages in rock layers is called biostratigraphy. Magnetostratigraphy examines data about changes in detrital remanent magnetism (DRM) at the time rocks were formed.

33. C: In geochronology, an eon is the longest time period, lasting at least half a billion years. An era lasts several hundred million years, an epoch measures tens of millions of years, and an age is shorter than 10 million years but longer than one million years.

34. C: In his 1924 work, The Origin of Life, Alexander Oparin argued that life arose on Earth through a "primordial soup" that is no longer possible because of atmospheric oxygen.

35. B: The most severe mass extinction event in Earth's history was the Permian-Triassic Event. It occurred approximately 251.4 million years ago, and resulted in the extinction of 96 percent of all marine species and 70 percent of terrestrial vertebrate species.

36. D: The Cambrian Explosion is best described as the dramatic increase in biodiversity that began about 530 million years ago and resulted in the emergence of complex animals over a period of millions of years. Evidence for this "explosion" of life comes mainly from fossil records. There are many possible explanations for it, ranging from an increase in oxygen levels to the development of eyes.

37. C: The Cosmological Principle is best described as a working assumption that has testable structural consequences. The principle, which underlies existing cosmological theories, assumes that the view of the universe possessed by observers on Earth is not distorted by their observational location. The observable implications of this theory are homogeneity (the same types of observational evidence are available regardless of one's vantage point within the universe) and isotropy (the same observational evidence is available by looking in any given direction from a single vantage point).

38. D: The physical structure of the universe is thought to consist of filaments (walls of superclusters, clusters, and galaxies) that surround large, bubble-like voids. Filaments are the largest structures in the universe, with some forming huge structures like the Great Wall and the Sloan Great Wall.

39. A: The structure of the Milky Way galaxy is spiral, meaning it has curved "arms" stretching out from a central point. While spiral galaxies have a flat, disc-like appearance, elliptical galaxies are more three-dimensional and appear to be roughly the same shape regardless of the viewing angle.

40. A: The distance from the Earth to the Sun is equal to one astronomical unit (AU). An AU is equal to 93 million miles, and is far smaller than a light year or a parsec. A light year is defined as the distance light can travel in a vacuum in one year, and is equal to roughly 64,341 AU. A parsec is the parallax of one arcsecond, and is equal to 206.26×10^3astronomical units.

41. A: The stream of charged particles that escape the Sun's gravitational pull is called solar wind. Solar wind is composed primarily of protons and electrons, and these particles are deflected away from the Earth by its magnetic field. When stray particles do manage to enter the atmosphere, they cause the auroras (northern and southern lights) and geomagnetic storms that can affect power grids.

42. D: The asteroid belt in our solar system is located between Mars and Jupiter. The asteroid belt is populated by asteroids and dwarf planets that are distributed thinly enough that spacecraft can pass though the belt with relative ease.

43. B: A total solar eclipse can be observed only by viewers located within the umbra. The umbra is the darkest part of the shadow, and the light source is not visible from it. The penumbra is the lighter portion of the shadow from which the light source is partially visible. In a solar eclipse, the Moon passes between the Earth and the Sun, and viewers in the umbra experience a total solar eclipse.

44. B: The main distinction between the isotopes carbon-12 and carbon-13 is that they have different mass numbers. Isotopes of a given element all have the same atomic number, since atomic number (also known as proton number) is the defining characteristic of each element. However, they have different neutron numbers, which causes them to have varying mass numbers as well. Both carbon-12 and carbon-13 are stable isotopes, meaning they do not experience observable radioactive decay.

45. A: Chemical compounds are formed when valence electrons from atoms of two different elements are shared or transferred. Valence electrons are the electrons located in the outermost shell of the atom, and they occupy the highest energy level. Atoms may form compounds by sharing valence electrons (covalent bonding) or by transferring electrons.

46. B: A closed thermodynamic system can exchange heat and work, but not matter, with its surrounding environment. In contrast, an isolated system cannot exchange heat, work, or matter with its surrounding environment, so its mass and energy levels always remain constant. Open systems can exchange heat, work, and mass with their surrounding environments.

47. B: The first law of classical thermodynamics states that energy can neither be created nor destroyed. The zeroth law is concerned with thermodynamic equilibrium, and the second and third laws discuss entropy.

48. A: The correct formula for converting Fahrenheit measurements to Celsius measurements is $5/9\ (F - 32)$, where F is the temperature in Fahrenheit.

49. A: Commercial nuclear reactors generate electricity through the process of nuclear fission. The fission process is used to heat water, which in turn generates steam that is used to produce electricity. This process is controlled to ensure safety, but it does produce nuclear waste that requires the use of extensive procedures to dispose of it safely.

50. B: Random error could be caused by extraneous disturbances that cannot be controlled. Random error is that which does not affect experimental results in a consistent, patterned way. In contrast, systematic error affects all experimental results consistently. For example, if an instrument is calibrated improperly, all experimental results will be skewed in the same direction.

How to Overcome Test Anxiety

Just the thought of taking a test is enough to make most people a little nervous. A test is an important event that can have a long-term impact on your future, so it's important to take it seriously and it's natural to feel anxious about performing well. But just because anxiety is normal, that doesn't mean that it's helpful in test taking, or that you should simply accept it as part of your life. Anxiety can have a variety of effects. These effects can be mild, like making you feel slightly nervous, or severe, like blocking your ability to focus or remember even a simple detail.

If you experience test anxiety—whether severe or mild—it's important to know how to beat it. To discover this, first you need to understand what causes test anxiety.

Causes of Test Anxiety

While we often think of anxiety as an uncontrollable emotional state, it can actually be caused by simple, practical things. One of the most common causes of test anxiety is that a person does not feel adequately prepared for their test. This feeling can be the result of many different issues such as poor study habits or lack of organization, but the most common culprit is time management. Starting to study too late, failing to organize your study time to cover all of the material, or being distracted while you study will mean that you're not well prepared for the test. This may lead to cramming the night before, which will cause you to be physically and mentally exhausted for the test. Poor time management also contributes to feelings of stress, fear, and hopelessness as you realize you are not well prepared but don't know what to do about it.

Other times, test anxiety is not related to your preparation for the test but comes from unresolved fear. This may be a past failure on a test, or poor performance on tests in general. It may come from comparing yourself to others who seem to be performing better or from the stress of living up to expectations. Anxiety may be driven by fears of the future—how failure on this test would affect your educational and career goals. These fears are often completely irrational, but they can still negatively impact your test performance.

Elements of Test Anxiety

As mentioned earlier, test anxiety is considered to be an emotional state, but it has physical and mental components as well. Sometimes you may not even realize that you are suffering from test anxiety until you notice the physical symptoms. These can include trembling hands, rapid heartbeat, sweating, nausea, and tense muscles. Extreme anxiety may lead to fainting or vomiting. Obviously, any of these symptoms can have a negative impact on testing. It is important to recognize them as soon as they begin to occur so that you can address the problem before it damages your performance.

The mental components of test anxiety include trouble focusing and inability to remember learned information. During a test, your mind is on high alert, which can help you recall information and stay focused for an extended period of time. However, anxiety interferes with your mind's natural processes, causing you to blank out, even on the questions you know well. The strain of testing during anxiety makes it difficult to stay focused, especially on a test that may take several hours. Extreme anxiety can take a huge mental toll, making it difficult not only to recall test information but even to understand the test questions or pull your thoughts together.

Effects of Test Anxiety

Test anxiety is like a disease—if left untreated, it will get progressively worse. Anxiety leads to poor performance, and this reinforces the feelings of fear and failure, which in turn lead to poor performances on subsequent tests. It can grow from a mild nervousness to a crippling condition. If allowed to progress, test anxiety can have a big impact on your schooling, and consequently on your future.

Test anxiety can spread to other parts of your life. Anxiety on tests can become anxiety in any stressful situation, and blanking on a test can turn into panicking in a job situation. But fortunately, you don't have to let anxiety rule your testing and determine your grades. There are a number of relatively simple steps you can take to move past anxiety and function normally on a test and in the rest of life.

Physical Steps for Beating Test Anxiety

While test anxiety is a serious problem, the good news is that it can be overcome. It doesn't have to control your ability to think and remember information. While it may take time, you can begin taking steps today to beat anxiety.

Just as your first hint that you may be struggling with anxiety comes from the physical symptoms, the first step to treating it is also physical. Rest is crucial for having a clear, strong mind. If you are tired, it is much easier to give in to anxiety. But if you establish good sleep habits, your body and mind will be ready to perform optimally, without the strain of exhaustion. Additionally, sleeping well helps you to retain information better, so you're more likely to recall the answers when you see the test questions.

Getting good sleep means more than going to bed on time. It's important to allow your brain time to relax. Take study breaks from time to time so it doesn't get overworked, and don't study right before bed. Take time to rest your mind before trying to rest your body, or you may find it difficult to fall asleep.

Along with sleep, other aspects of physical health are important in preparing for a test. Good nutrition is vital for good brain function. Sugary foods and drinks may give a burst of energy but this burst is followed by a crash, both physically and emotionally. Instead, fuel your body with protein and vitamin-rich foods.

Also, drink plenty of water. Dehydration can lead to headaches and exhaustion, especially if your brain is already under stress from the rigors of the test. Particularly if your test is a long one, drink water during the breaks. And if possible, take an energy-boosting snack to eat between sections.

Along with sleep and diet, a third important part of physical health is exercise. Maintaining a steady workout schedule is helpful, but even taking 5-minute study breaks to walk can help get your blood pumping faster and clear your head. Exercise also releases endorphins, which contribute to a positive feeling and can help combat test anxiety.

When you nurture your physical health, you are also contributing to your mental health. If your body is healthy, your mind is much more likely to be healthy as well. So take time to rest, nourish your body with healthy food and water, and get moving as much as possible. Taking these physical steps will make you stronger and more able to take the mental steps necessary to overcome test anxiety.

Mental Steps for Beating Test Anxiety

Working on the mental side of test anxiety can be more challenging, but as with the physical side, there are clear steps you can take to overcome it. As mentioned earlier, test anxiety often stems from lack of preparation, so the obvious solution is to prepare for the test. Effective studying may be the most important weapon you have for beating test anxiety, but you can and should employ several other mental tools to combat fear.

First, boost your confidence by reminding yourself of past success—tests or projects that you aced. If you're putting as much effort into preparing for this test as you did for those, there's no reason you should expect to fail here. Work hard to prepare; then trust your preparation.

Second, surround yourself with encouraging people. It can be helpful to find a study group, but be sure that the people you're around will encourage a positive attitude. If you spend time with others who are anxious or cynical, this will only contribute to your own anxiety. Look for others who are motivated to study hard from a desire to succeed, not from a fear of failure.

Third, reward yourself. A test is physically and mentally tiring, even without anxiety, and it can be helpful to have something to look forward to. Plan an activity following the test, regardless of the outcome, such as going to a movie or getting ice cream.

When you are taking the test, if you find yourself beginning to feel anxious, remind yourself that you know the material. Visualize successfully completing the test. Then take a few deep, relaxing breaths and return to it. Work through the questions carefully but with confidence, knowing that you are capable of succeeding.

Developing a healthy mental approach to test taking will also aid in other areas of life. Test anxiety affects more than just the actual test—it can be damaging to your mental health and even contribute to depression. It's important to beat test anxiety before it becomes a problem for more than testing.

Study Strategy

Being prepared for the test is necessary to combat anxiety, but what does being prepared look like? You may study for hours on end and still not feel prepared. What you need is a strategy for test prep. The next few pages outline our recommended steps to help you plan out and conquer the challenge of preparation.

Step 1: Scope Out the Test

Learn everything you can about the format (multiple choice, essay, etc.) and what will be on the test. Gather any study materials, course outlines, or sample exams that may be available. Not only will this help you to prepare, but knowing what to expect can help to alleviate test anxiety.

Step 2: Map Out the Material

Look through the textbook or study guide and make note of how many chapters or sections it has. Then divide these over the time you have. For example, if a book has 15 chapters and you have five days to study, you need to cover three chapters each day. Even better, if you have the time, leave an extra day at the end for overall review after you have gone through the material in depth.

If time is limited, you may need to prioritize the material. Look through it and make note of which sections you think you already have a good grasp on, and which need review. While you are studying, skim quickly through the familiar sections and take more time on the challenging parts.

Write out your plan so you don't get lost as you go. Having a written plan also helps you feel more in control of the study, so anxiety is less likely to arise from feeling overwhelmed at the amount to cover.

Step 3: Gather Your Tools

Decide what study method works best for you. Do you prefer to highlight in the book as you study and then go back over the highlighted portions? Or do you type out notes of the important information? Or is it helpful to make flashcards that you can carry with you? Assemble the pens, index cards, highlighters, post-it notes, and any other materials you may need so you won't be distracted by getting up to find things while you study.

If you're having a hard time retaining the information or organizing your notes, experiment with different methods. For example, try color-coding by subject with colored pens, highlighters, or post-it notes. If you learn better by hearing, try recording yourself reading your notes so you can listen while in the car, working out, or simply sitting at your desk. Ask a friend to quiz you from your flashcards, or try teaching someone the material to solidify it in your mind.

Step 4: Create Your Environment

It's important to avoid distractions while you study. This includes both the obvious distractions like visitors and the subtle distractions like an uncomfortable chair (or a too-comfortable couch that makes you want to fall asleep). Set up the best study environment possible: good lighting and a comfortable work area. If background music helps you focus, you may want to turn it on, but otherwise keep the room quiet. If you are using a computer to take notes, be sure you don't have any other windows open, especially applications like social media, games, or anything else that could distract you. Silence your phone and turn off notifications. Be sure to keep water close by so you stay hydrated while you study (but avoid unhealthy drinks and snacks).

Also, take into account the best time of day to study. Are you freshest first thing in the morning? Try to set aside some time then to work through the material. Is your mind clearer in the afternoon or evening? Schedule your study session then. Another method is to study at the same time of day that you will take the test, so that your brain gets used to working on the material at that time and will be ready to focus at test time.

Step 5: Study!

Once you have done all the study preparation, it's time to settle into the actual studying. Sit down, take a few moments to settle your mind so you can focus, and begin to follow your study plan. Don't give in to distractions or let yourself procrastinate. This is your time to prepare so you'll be ready to fearlessly approach the test. Make the most of the time and stay focused.

Of course, you don't want to burn out. If you study too long you may find that you're not retaining the information very well. Take regular study breaks. For example, taking five minutes out of every hour to walk briskly, breathing deeply and swinging your arms, can help your mind stay fresh.

As you get to the end of each chapter or section, it's a good idea to do a quick review. Remind yourself of what you learned and work on any difficult parts. When you feel that you've mastered the material, move on to the next part. At the end of your study session, briefly skim through your notes again.

But while review is helpful, cramming last minute is NOT. If at all possible, work ahead so that you won't need to fit all your study into the last day. Cramming overloads your brain with more information than it can process and retain, and your tired mind may struggle to recall even previously learned information when it is overwhelmed with last-minute study. Also, the urgent nature of cramming and the stress placed on your brain contribute to anxiety. You'll be more likely to go to the test feeling unprepared and having trouble thinking clearly.

So don't cram, and don't stay up late before the test, even just to review your notes at a leisurely pace. Your brain needs rest more than it needs to go over the information again. In fact, plan to finish your studies by noon or early afternoon the day before the test. Give your brain the rest of the day to relax or focus on other things, and get a good night's sleep. Then you will be fresh for the test and better able to recall what you've studied.

Step 6: Take a Practice Test

Many courses offer sample tests, either online or in the study materials. This is an excellent resource to check whether you have mastered the material, as well as to prepare for the test format and environment.

Check the test format ahead of time: the number of questions, the type (multiple choice, free response, etc.), and the time limit. Then create a plan for working through them. For example, if you have 30 minutes to take a 60-question test, your limit is 30 seconds per question. Spend less time on the questions you know well so that you can take more time on the difficult ones.

If you have time to take several practice tests, take the first one open book, with no time limit. Work through the questions at your own pace and make sure you fully understand them. Gradually work up to taking a test under test conditions: sit at a desk with all study materials put away and set a timer. Pace yourself to make sure you finish the test with time to spare and go back to check your answers if you have time.

After each test, check your answers. On the questions you missed, be sure you understand why you missed them. Did you misread the question (tests can use tricky wording)? Did you forget the information? Or was it something you hadn't learned? Go back and study any shaky areas that the practice tests reveal.

Taking these tests not only helps with your grade, but also aids in combating test anxiety. If you're already used to the test conditions, you're less likely to worry about it, and working through tests until you're scoring well gives you a confidence boost. Go through the practice tests until you feel comfortable, and then you can go into the test knowing that you're ready for it.

Test Tips

On test day, you should be confident, knowing that you've prepared well and are ready to answer the questions. But aside from preparation, there are several test day strategies you can employ to maximize your performance.

First, as stated before, get a good night's sleep the night before the test (and for several nights before that, if possible). Go into the test with a fresh, alert mind rather than staying up late to study.

Try not to change too much about your normal routine on the day of the test. It's important to eat a nutritious breakfast, but if you normally don't eat breakfast at all, consider eating just a protein bar. If you're a coffee drinker, go ahead and have your normal coffee. Just make sure you time it so that the caffeine doesn't wear off right in the middle of your test. Avoid sugary beverages, and drink enough water to stay hydrated but not so much that you need a restroom break 10 minutes into the test. If your test isn't first thing in the morning, consider going for a walk or doing a light workout before the test to get your blood flowing.

Allow yourself enough time to get ready, and leave for the test with plenty of time to spare so you won't have the anxiety of scrambling to arrive in time. Another reason to be early is to select a good seat. It's helpful to sit away from doors and windows, which can be distracting. Find a good seat, get out your supplies, and settle your mind before the test begins.

When the test begins, start by going over the instructions carefully, even if you already know what to expect. Make sure you avoid any careless mistakes by following the directions.

Then begin working through the questions, pacing yourself as you've practiced. If you're not sure on an answer, don't spend too much time on it, and don't let it shake your confidence. Either skip it and come back later, or eliminate as many wrong answers as possible and guess among the remaining ones. Don't dwell on these questions as you continue—put them out of your mind and focus on what lies ahead.

Be sure to read all of the answer choices, even if you're sure the first one is the right answer. Sometimes you'll find a better one if you keep reading. But don't second-guess yourself if you do immediately know the answer. Your gut instinct is usually right. Don't let test anxiety rob you of the information you know.

If you have time at the end of the test (and if the test format allows), go back and review your answers. Be cautious about changing any, since your first instinct tends to be correct, but make sure you didn't misread any of the questions or accidentally mark the wrong answer choice. Look over any you skipped and make an educated guess.

At the end, leave the test feeling confident. You've done your best, so don't waste time worrying about your performance or wishing you could change anything. Instead, celebrate the successful completion of this test. And finally, use this test to learn how to deal with anxiety even better next time.

Review Video: Test Anxiety
Visit mometrix.com/academy and enter code: 100340

Important Qualification

Not all anxiety is created equal. If your test anxiety is causing major issues in your life beyond the classroom or testing center, or if you are experiencing troubling physical symptoms related to your anxiety, it may be a sign of a serious physiological or psychological condition. If this sounds like your situation, we strongly encourage you to seek professional help.

Online Resources

Due to our efforts to try to keep this book to a manageable length, we've created a link that will give you access to all of your online resources:

mometrix.com/resources719/ssregearthsci

It's Your Moment, Let's Celebrate It!

Share your story @mometrixtestpreparation